Management Observation
and Communication Theory

Management Observation and Communication Theory

Heikki Heiskanen
and G. A. Swanson

Q

Quorum Books
Westport, Connecticut / London

Library of Congress Cataloging-in-Publication Data

Heiskanen, Heikki.
  Management observation and communication theory / Heikki Heiskanen
and G. A. Swanson.
      p.   cm.
  Includes index.
  ISBN 0–89930–637–3
  1. Management—Philosophy.   2. Communication in management.
3. System theory.   I. Swanson, G. A.   II. Title.
HD30.19.H45   1992
658.4'5—dc20   91–48120

British Library Cataloguing in Publication Data is available.

Library of Congress Catalog Card Number: 91–48120
ISBN: 0–89930–637–3

First published in 1992

Quorum Books, 88 Post Road West, Westport, CT 06881
An imprint of Greenwood Publishing Group, Inc.

Printed in the United States of America

The paper used in this book complies with the
Permanent Paper Standard issued by the National
Information Standards Organization (Z39.48–1984).

10 9 8 7 6 5 4 3 2 1

Copyright Acknowledgment
The authors and publisher gratefully acknowledge permission
to use the following: Extracts from *Living Systems*, by James G. Miller,
McGraw-Hill, Inc., 1978. Reprinted with permission of McGraw-Hill, Inc.

Contents

Figures and Tables   vii

Preface   xi

1 Introduction and Overview   1

2 Elements of Living Systems Theory   15

3 Elements of Linguistic-Mathematical Theory   31

4 How to Construct Backdrops   51

5 How to Use Backdrops in Management   75

6 The Big Picture: Combinations of Analysis Results   95

7 Syntactic Analysis and Its Methods   105

8 Semantic Analysis   129

9 An Overview of Some Semantic Methods   155

10 Summary   177

Index   183

Figures and Tables

Figures

1.1	Resource Administration Cube	5
1.2	Linguistic-Mathematical Theory	7
3.1	Systems Theory Ideas as a Hierarchy	34
3.2	Basic Ideas of L-M Theory	36
3.3	Theories in the Form of a Hierarchy	39
3.4	Basic Concepts of the Social Sciences, Computers, and Mathematics and Their Counterparts in Systems Theory	43
3.5	Domain of Qualitative and Mathematical Methods	46
3.6	Propositions Expressed in Value, Variable, and Entity Language	48
4.1	Organization of an Original Set of Observations into Mutually Exclusive Sets, i.e., Dimensions or Variables	53
4.2	Values of Variables Covering the Scope of Possible States from the Minimal to the Maximal States	54
4.3	How People Observe, Compare Observations with Objectives, Evaluate Their Worth, and Decide What Responses Are Deserved	57
4.4	Formulation of Observations as Estimates and as Measurements	59
4.5	Similarities and Distinctions Between the Part and Membership Hierarchies	61
4.6	Measuring Units in the Form of a Hierarchy	62
4.7	Description of a State of Time	63
4.8	Hierarchy of Variables	65
4.9	Organizing Entities	68
4.10	Entity Hierarchy as an Aggregate Hierarchy	70
4.11	Activity of a Company as a Process Hierarchy, in which the Individual Jobs Are the Elements	71
4.12	Individual Persons as a Membership Hierarchy	72
5.1	A Source System	77
5.2	Backdrop Supporting Variables	79

5.3	An Element Observation	81
5.4	Data Matrix Construction	82
5.5	A Data Matrix	83
5.6	A Coexistence Pair	84
5.7	Combining Pairs into Rows	85
5.8	A Row of Coexistence Pairs on a Set of Coordinates	87
5.9	Deviations from Primary Rule	88
5.10	Investigating Higher-Level Generalized Rules	89
5.11	A Disparity Pair	91
5.12	Disparity Rows	92
6.1	A Value Model	96
6.2	Variable Model	97
6.3	A Variable Star	98
6.4	A Variable Model of Stars	98
6.5	An Entity Model	99
6.6	Distributive Bases as a Variable Hierarchy	101
6.7	A Concept Card	103
7.1	Syntactic Method of L-M Theory	108
7.2	Hierarchy of Systems Theory Concepts	109
7.3	Compilations Hierarchy	109
7.4	Linguistic Syntactic Analysis	111
7.5	Syntactic Graph	112
7.6	Semantic or Cognitive Network	113
7.7	Element Hierarchy Concerning William	113
7.8	Table of Linked Elements	115
7.9	N-SIM-Method	118
7.10	Examples of Graphs	119
7.11	Coordinative Method for Social Policy Target Programs	123
7.12	A Weighted-Ends Tree	124
7.13	Syntactic Methods Compared with L-M Theory	126
8.1	Definition of a Concept	130
8.2	Definitions in Spatiotemporal and Conceptual Space	132
8.3	Definition Hierarchy Constructed from Top Down	133
8.4	A Definition Table	136
8.5	A Definition Elementary Network	136
8.6a–c	Combining Elementary Networks	136–137
8.7	A Network of Definitions: A Compilation for Descriptive Definitions	138
8.8	Vocabulary Structure	140

8.9	Minimum Mental Effort	141
8.10	Need for Definitions	142
8.11	A Pairwise Comparison of Definitions	143
8.12	Tabular Comparison	144
8.13	Comparison of Various Definitions of Content Analysis	146
8.14	A Standardized Definition	148
8.15	A Refined Definition, Defining the Concept Both Descriptively and Enumeratively	150
8.16	Analysis of a Verbal Scale	151
8.17	Analysis Results of a Verbal Scale in the Form of a Variable and Value Model	152
9.1	Semantic Thinking in a Nutshell	156
9.2	Ingredients of Meaning	158
9.3	Comparison of Words Close to Bachelor by Means of Shared Features	162
9.4	A Hierarchy of Concepts in the Semantic Memory of Quillian	163
9.5	Semantic Profiles of the Semantic Differential Technique	164
9.6	Comparison of Words Close to Bachelor by Means of Semantic Differential Technique	165
9.7	A Set as an Elementary Hierarchy	166
9.8	Structuralist Interpretations of Sememes Close to Bachelor	167
9.9	A Semantic Hierarchy for Presenting Meanings of Markers and Distinguishers	168
9.10	Comparison of Semantic Methods by Means of the Concepts They Employ	170
9.11	A Simultaneous Presentation of Descriptive Definitions and Hierarchic Organization of Respective Concepts	174

Tables

1.1	Hierarchy of Living Systems	3
2.1	Components of the 19 Critical Subsystems of an Organization	19

Preface

We have written this book to begin to satisfy a fundamental need in management theory. Management theory needs a global systemic conceptual framework that instructs the development of organization-specific management theories. Organizations evolve by specialization and integration. Attempting to fit all organizations in the same theory with slight variations ignores the latest evolutionary developments in particular organizations. Such attempts are reactionary and not progressive.

Linguistic-mathematical theory is a pure system. It is defined by the interrelationships of its own elements and is not dependent on any particular empirical element. This global conceptual framework can be used to examine communications within organizations to discover the relationships and interactions in their concrete processes. Customized management theories may be synthesized from that information. The concepts that comprise linguistic-mathematical theory have been used extensively for this purpose by coauthor Heiskanen over many years. Many of the specific techniques described in this book were developed from that practical application.

Organizations are living systems—higher-order human systems. Management is the most important element of an organization's decider subsystem, which makes decisions and processes information that controls its concrete operations. The decider subsystem is served by several other information-processing subsystems. Because of the ever-increasing complexity of modern societies and organizations, the information that informs and controls organizations cannot always be casually observed and used. Management communication and observation theory provides the means to document and formalize that information. While we make no claims to have provided the ultimate global conceptual framework, we believe this book is a step in the right direction.

1

Introduction and Overview

Every manager has a theory about some aspect of management, and often different theories about different aspects. Seldom do managers worry much about whether those theories are complementary or conflicting, or how the theories relate in detail. Important items may be overlooked. As a result, what happens within organizations may be as surprising as what happens in their environments. Management observation and communication theory can minimize the occurrence of such surprises.

CONCRETE PROCESS MANAGEMENT

Over the twentieth century, a broad set of ideas and procedures were brought together under such captions as MBO (management by objectives), MBR (management by results), and OOO (objective-oriented organization). Some of those ideas and procedures recently have been questioned on the grounds of effective management.

A glaring weakness of MBO is that it implies that meeting objectives constitutes success. If objectives could be formulated on perfect knowledge about the future, that criterion of success might be useful. In the uncertain future faced by managers, however, meeting objectives describes failure as often as it describes success.

The fundamental problem with MBO is that information about the concrete processes being managed may be disconnected conveniently from the management process. Objectives typically are stated in quite abstract or very limited terms. Meeting such objectives does not ensure that the concrete processes of organizations are controlled effectively and efficiently by management.

Management observation and communication theory connects information

1

about objectives to information about the concrete processes of organizations. It insists that the results (the concrete processes) brought about by management decisions be evaluated by using the measurements of those results when possible, and by using quantitative and qualitative assessments when measurements are not available.

This way of viewing management is built on linguistic-mathematical theory (L-M theory) (Heiskanen 1975; Heiskanen and Airaksinen 1979). That theory recognizes a close relationship between the logics of linguistic systems and numerical ones. It uses hierarchical analyses to connect the many rather abstract notions of management incorporated in statements of objectives to the empirically observable concrete processes of organizations.

External goals (often termed *objectives*) of organizations may be pursued only to the extent that they correspond in some degree to the organization's internal purposes. MBO too often fails to connect external goals to the internal functions of organizations. That failure may be overcome by using L-M theory to synthesize information about internal processes into purposes and to connect the resulting general statements to similarly general statements about an organization's external goals.

The perspective of management observation and communication theory is always concrete systems, which are nonrandom accumulations of matter, energy, and information in a region of physical space and time—real physical things, the stuff we bump into. Because it focuses on organizations, management observation and communication theory concerns a special subset of all concrete systems—the living ones. Living systems theory (LST) is a conceptual framework that views the entire domain of systems from the perspective of living systems (Miller 1978). Types of living systems may be arranged on a hierarchy from the simplest to the most complex. Eight types are identified in Table 1.1. All of those types of systems must perform certain critical, concrete processes to continue to exist in earth's environment.

Management observation and communication theory incorporates LST for the following reasons:

1. The perspective of LST is concrete systems.
2. LST is a conceptual framework that integrates knowledge from most disciplinal sciences into a coherent whole.
3. LST is stated in sufficient detail to aid applied management.
4. The LST view of organizations likely is little biased by management perceptions and thus provides a backdrop for evaluating those perceptions.
5. LST is developed with systems thinking.

The focus of any management theory is the decider subsystem of mainly organizations. Miller defines the decider subsystem as the "executive subsystem

Table 1.1
Hierarchy of Living Systems

1.	Cells	Minute unitary masses of intricately organized protoplasm. "All living systems either are free-living cells or have cells as their least complex living components" (Miller 1978: 203).
2.	Organs	Organism subsystems that are formed from tissues. Tissues are collections "of adjacent cells of like origin and structure which carry out similar, specialized processes" (Miller 1978: 315).
3.	Organism	Any animal or plant with organs and parts that function together to maintain life.
4.	Group	"A set of single organisms, commonly called members, which, over a period of time or multiple interrupted periods, relate to one another face-to-face, processing matter-energy and information" (Miller 1978: 515).
5.	Organizations	Concrete living systems with multiechelon deciders whose components and subsystems may be subsidiary organizations, groups, and (uncommonly) single persons (Miller 1978: 595).
6.	Communities	Higher-order human systems prominently composed of both organizations and individual persons as subsystems. They have governmental organizations that are given special powers to control their components.
7.	Societies	"Large, living, concrete systems with organizations and lower levels of living systems as subsystems and components" (Miller 1978: 747).
8.	Supranational Systems	Concrete, living systems "composed of two or more societies, some or all of whose processes are under the control of a decider that is superordinated to their highest echelons" (Miller 1978: 903).

that receives information inputs from all other subsystems and transmits to them outputs for guidance, coordination, and control of the system" (1978: 3).

The common terms for this subsystem are *management* and *administration*. *Management* is used generally in business and industrial organizations, and *administration* in other types of economic organizations such as governments and universities. The principles and procedures of management observation and communication theory are equally applicable to both types of organizations.

TOO MANY MANAGEMENT THEORIES?

Managers conceptualize theories in response to perplexing questions that arise during hands-on management experience. Perplexing questions concern complex situations. Every day managers of modern organizations are faced with a sea of complexity. A grand theory is needed to integrate the many special-purpose theories arising in management practice.

Actually, many theories with a broad application to the various aspects of management practice are published. They typically integrate several special-purpose theories. However, they ordinarily do not provide the means to select a set of special-purpose theories for integration into a coherent general theory. Often the proponents of a particular mosaic of special theories can justify its components only by claiming that they are needed to make the theory comprehensive.

New integrations of well-known special-purpose theories arise frequently. They commonly emphasize a few aspects of the special-purpose theories to which managers are not giving much attention. The repackaged theories are named to reflect the emphasis, and the so-called new theory is published with an aura of grand discovery applicable to virtually every organization.

Many such theories reflect how individual managers or management teams were successful in particular situations. A theory's historical success and wide publication, in fact, makes it unlikely to produce future successes. Seldom do such situations remain unchanged over time. Competing managers build strategies to overcome the advantages gained by past successful managers.

The world does not need another rehashed management theory making global claims. It needs a theory for integrating special-purpose theories that have been proven useful into customized mosaics that fit the varying cultures of modern organizations.

L-M theory is such a theory of theories. We use it to construct a theory of management observation and communication that views organizations as concrete systems. Different managers may use it to construct general theories that do not necessarily incorporate the concrete systems view.

ART OF MANAGEMENT

In some sense, the term *management science* is a misnomer. Science searches for laws—the constant, the repeatable. Management is art. Art elicits emotion, a holistic, greater essence than that possessed by its discoverable parts. It is elusive. It is creative. Management success or failure may depend as much on the draw of the card as on a manager's philosophy or style.

Notwithstanding the elusive nature of management, mastering management propaedeutics increases the odds of success. In some sense, it is possible to learn the art of management. Artists are both born and made.

Both art and science are expressions of living systems and, thus, mediated by concrete processes. One seldom, if ever, exists without the other. This book concerns integrating what science is learning about concrete processes into the art of management. Thus, it concerns the media in which the art is exercised.

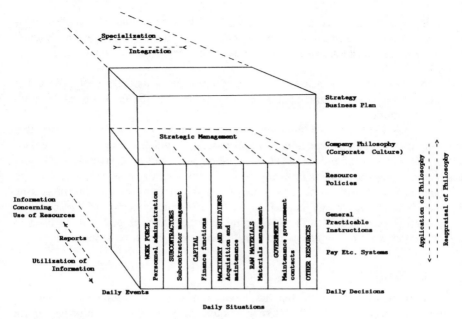

Figure 1.1
Resource Administration Cube

A painter masters the variations in the color spectrum, the textures of paints and canvases, the relative sizes of objects, perspective, and so forth. The media that modern managers must master are far more complex, involving dynamic interacting processes.

Figure 1.1, the Resource Administration Cube, is a simplified illustration of that complexity. Daily events are at the forefront. These events are controlled by information processes that formalize them into effective reports. Both specialization and integration exist among different administrative functions, and every function is both a hierarchical reduction of the strategy of management and a contribution to the whole. Mastering such complexity is an extremely demanding job and is, in fact, nearly impossible.

SIMPLIFICATION

Managers overcome the nearly impossible by devising ways to simplify their perceptions of the complexities they encounter. Forming theories is one way managers simplify perceptions of complex situations. Their different theories, however, are not always formed of ideas that may be restated in terms of one another.

Systems thinking is another way to simplify perceptions of complex situations. Using it, ideas are stated in a manner such that they can always be restated in terms of other ideas, because virtually all ideas can be stated in terms of systems.

A *system* is any set of related and interacting elements. That very general but nontrivial idea has been used to simplify complexities in practically every modern discipline.

In this book systems thinking is used to build an integrating theory that simplifies our perceptions of the complex media in which managers exercise their art. Our theory of management observation and communication is linguistic-mathematical because it integrates information expressed in symbols of both languages and mathematical systems. The systemic concepts of the integrating theory, L-M theory, are connected to the systemic concepts of the concrete processes provided in LST, developing a set of theories that can be used to customize a set of management microtheories to a particular organization.

L-M THEORY

L-M theory is a conceptual framework that integrates judgmental linguistic information with both qualitative and quantitative numerical information for management use. It provides a means to simplify managers' perceptions of complex situations.

As its name implies, L-M theory identifies factors that are fundamental components of symbolic conceptual systems, both numerical and linguistic. Such factors may be used to analyze and synthesize the information flows of organizations. Managers control organizations through a set of information-processing (communication) subsystems. L-M theory may be used to formulate conventional meanings using the information flows in organizations themselves. Those meanings, consequently, are understood throughout the respective organizations. L-M theory also may be used to discover the meanings of communications among organizations and their suprasystem societies. Figure 1.2 outlines the theory.

It is important to recognize at the outset that L-M theory concerns information about information. It queries the information in the organization from a higher conceptual vantage point—knowledge of fundamental components of symbolic systems. The organizational information examined may be practical or esoteric, epistomological or pedagogical, or even logical or philosophical. L-M theory does not change the basic character of the concepts it examines. Because it queries information, L-M theory obviously cannot be demonstrated apart from organizational information.

Another important aspect of L-M theory arises from its applicability to both local and global information. Because it can be applied to all sorts of informa-

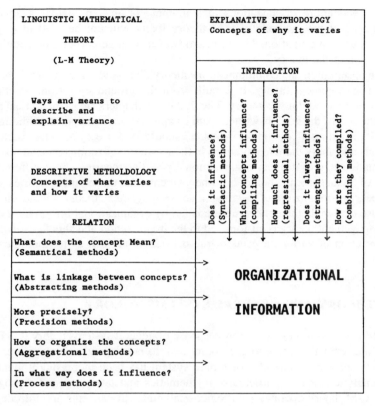

Figure 1.2
Linguistic-Mathematical Theory

tion, L-M theory can be used to integrate a particular global conceptual framework into the information processes of organizations. It may be used to view organizations, as LST does, to form customized management theories incorporating the specific purposes and goals of particular organizations. To do so, we view the organization from the LST perspective as we investigate its information.

L-M theory is quite comprehensive and includes many methods. We offer it as a means of simplifying managers' perceptions of the very complex existence of organizations. At first glance, managers may react negatively. The last thing they need is to figure out another complex system.

Two things should be considered in that regard. A system that reduces the perceived complexity of another very complex system while maintaining its integrity must comprehend that system. Managers themselves ordinarily do not comprehend entire organizations at a moment or in a particular analysis or synthesis. All the methods of L-M theory likely will not be used in a single management investigation. Over time, however, a large corporation should use all aspects of the theory.

The observation and communications theory discussed throughout this book is truly a management theory. It is built from the ground up—from practice to method to methodology to theory. The first three chapters are as theoretical as we get. The rest of the book is written from an applications standpoint. Although we are not providing a cookbook, managers should find it easy to select particular methods and apply them to situations in their own organizations. As the resulting information aggregates, an organizations' peculiar theories about different aspects of management should become evident. As those microtheories come together, an organizations' peculiar macromanagement theory should emerge. Because the whole theoretic structure is fed by organizational information itself, the management theory is customized to the organization and should evolve with the evolution of various aspects of the organization, such as technological advances.

L-M THEORY AND GENERAL SYSTEMS THEORY

L-M theory is a pure system in the sense of general systems theory (GST). Its terms are defined relative to each other and do not depend on any reference to concrete substance. The idea of a pure system has been increasingly identified with analytic science, particularly mathematics and lately computer programming. L-M theory operates with logico-mathematical concepts and introduces a way to restate linguistic concepts into them.

The idea of a pure system should be clarified. A brief overview of its development helps put it into perspective. During the first half of the twentieth century, three separate disciplines contributed significantly to developing the idea of viewing existence in terms of systems.

Einstein, Lorentz, and Minkowski (Einstein 1961) formulated relativity theory in physics. They identified the relationships among the three dimensions of physical space and a fourth dimension, time, demonstrating that understanding the relationships among system components is crucial to understanding both components and systems.

In somewhat parallel developments, scientists in biology and psychology formulated open systems theory. Kohler (1921, 1927, 1938) formulated it out of Gestalt psychology, and von Bertalanffy (1950, 1956, 1968) arrived at it from the perspective of biological systems.

Open systems theory explains how concrete systems with relatively open boundaries can continue to exist indefinitely despite the limited existence imposed on relatively closed systems by the laws of thermodynamics. A vital aspect of both von Bertalanffy's and Kohler's formulations was Hill's (1931) idea of a dynamic steady state maintained by a continual expenditure of energy. Living systems such as the organizations controlled by managers are relatively open systems that continue to exist indefinitely.

By generalizing Gibbs's (1902) second law of thermodynamics from relatively closed systems to relatively open ones, methodologies for formulating exact mathematical relationships may be extended from physics to biology. Indeed, they may be extended to engineering, social sciences, and management as well. That very generalization implies the "formal correspondence of general principles, irrespective of the kind of relations or forces between components" (von Bertalanffy 1950: 29).

Patterns themselves may be significant and totally divorced from the elements and criteria of relationships that constitute a particular system. Such patterns are themselves systems. Arrangements in which types of relationships or forces and types of components may be varied without changing the arrangement were termed *pure systems* by von Bertalanffy. He called the scientific doctrine stating that such systems exist GST. Systems thinking emphasizes the importance of relationships and interactions among the parts of a perceived whole. GST provides a conceptual basis for extending methods of formalizing perceived relationships and interactions among scientific disciplines.

L-M theory is a pure system with reference to managers' theories and various kinds of assessments. Numerous special theories may be included in L-M theory. For example, different methods of semantical and syntactical linguistic analyses may be combined with hierarchy theory to construct a methodology for discovering nonquantifiable management standards for certain kinds of decisions.

L-M theory, consequently, is a metatheory. It integrates various management and scientific theories into a coherent whole to provide a means of customizing management theory to particular organizations. We use it with LST to form an integrative theory of observation and communication for customizing the management of concrete processes to particular organizations.

L-M theory need not be esoteric. We produce applied theory with it. We include component special theories that are directly applicable to practice, and in many cases they emerge directly from practice. Applied theory connects such comprehensive theories as LST and hierarchy theory with management theories, which in turn, connect with practice.

HIERARCHY THEORY AND THE THEORY OF MANAGEMENT OBSERVATION AND COMMUNICATION

Hierarchy theory differentiates levels of organizations using particular criteria. It makes no ontological claims. It is a very broad theory for epistomologically organizing concepts. Its central idea is that certain patterns or forces at higher hierarchical levels constrain or comprehend certain patterns or forces at lower levels.

Organizations, for example, have multiechelon decider subsystems that constitute a hierarchy based on the criterion of authority. The manager's span of control—the number of persons that a manager can control effectively—is limited. In a particular situation a line supervisor may control ten production workers and may be, in turn, one of eight supervisors controlled by a foreman. Although foremen are ultimately responsible for the entire production activity under them, they control it indirectly through the supervisors. The foremen's constraints are applied to supervisors, and supervisors in turn apply constraints to workers. The constraints are of two different kinds. The details that concern each level are also different.

Hierarchy theory puts such patterns forward as characteristic of one way among others that humans organize concepts about their existence. Management observation and communication theory incorporates the hierarchical pattern in analyzing and synthesizing various types of organizational and environmental information in L-M theory, and for structuring life in LST.

L-M THEORY, LST, AND HIERARCHY THEORY

Hierarchy theory concerns management observation and communication theory through both L-M theory and LST. Although L-M theory may be used to construct management theories based on any notion, it is especially compatible with LST and hierarchy theory because all three theories view existence as systems. LST, like L-M theory, incorporates hierarchy theory directly. Hierarchy theory, consequently, may be viewed as a general facilitator of the theory of management observation and communication.

Hierarchy theory's role in LST is discussed by Swanson and Miller (1989: 178). Hierarchy theory is a quantitative theory beginning to be given understood verbally expressed applications, and LST is a verbal theory beginning to be quantified. The central idea of hierarchy theory is a vital component of LST. Hierarchy theory states that levels of organization can be differentiated based on measurements made on a spatial temporal scale, for example, in terms of rate criteria and spatial criteria.

Some scientists view LST as an ontological theory. Miller, its author, makes no ontological claims. He simply asserts that concrete systems composed of matter, energy, and information are identifiably different from what he terms "abstracted systems." Concrete systems may be empirically confirmed, while abstracted systems cannot be. Consequently, hierarchy theory and LST are both systemic conceptual frameworks that organize human ideas. LST distinguishes between ideas that are empirically confirmable and those that are not. Hierarchy theory more or less relegates the question of empirical confirmation to methodology.

Those two global conceptual frameworks are brought to bear on management information by L-M theory, an integrating theory that concerns a common set of logic fundamental to symbolic systems both linguistic and numeric. In tandem, L-M theory, LST, and hierarchy theory comprise our theory of management observation and communication.

The complexity of organizations arises from the relationships and interactions of concrete system components and subsystems. Hierarchy theory and LST arrange the information about those complexities in ways that simplify it and clarify the interactions. Hierarchy theory concentrates on ways to simplify perceptions, and LST emphasizes ways to clarify concrete processes. L-M theory integrates an LST view of organizations, with the actual information generated in organizations used to produce a management theory supported by both methodology and particular methods.

NEED FOR AN INTEGRATIVE GENERAL THEORY

Historians will label the turn of the twenty-first century the "Information Revolution." The rapid acceleration of information technology is feeding a surge of other technological advances that, in turn, increasingly is making management the art of administering technological progress, both informational and other advances.

New technology is always the product of a relatively few specialists. Integrating new technology into organizations that are understood by both insiders and outsiders in the context of older technology is an extremely demanding job.

By nature of the hierarchical constraints that differentiate organizations from groups, managers naturally think in relatively grand terms. If higher-level managers thought about organizations in the same detail as lower-level managers, no organization would exist. Their ideas are generalizations of the detailed ideas of persons under their management. Because that natural condition exists in organizations, it is easy to disconnect the grand notions of managers from the concrete processes of organizations. The explosive technological environment exacerbates the situation, even though advances in information technology contain the means to mitigate it.

An integrative general theory of management is needed to connect the more general and, consequently, vague ideas of management to information contained in the concrete processes of organizations. It is needed to both differentiate and synthesize the massive amounts of information processed by modern organizations.

Increasing information may enlighten or confuse a receiver. Information overload and underload and misinformation may cause ineffective management decisions and actions.

Today the social science literature often does not distinguish clearly between measurements of concrete processes and their various interpretations. That blurred view has found its way into the management literature. Managers as a result often do not clearly distinguish between information from the concrete processes they manage and various notions about what that information means in some grand scheme. That situation confuses concrete process feedback with the hopes and goals of managers. Consequently, information about the success or failure of previous decisions, policies, and methods is diminished. No dynamic concrete system can function effectively without timely feedback. Management observation and communication theory connects the notions of managers with the information on concrete processes of organizations, placing both the dreams and the reality in perspective.

We believe at least five factors constitute the conditions necessary for the success of modern organizations: knowledge, a capacity for applying knowledge, a vision of the future, a spirit of enterprise, and capable management. Successful organizations know the state-of-the-art technology and economic conditions in their own fields and in their environments. They realize that technology and economic conditions change over time and participate in those changes by forecasting the future. Present knowledge and a vision of the future are connected by applying advancing knowledge to the firm. Implementing new technology and methods, adapting to changes within society, exploiting market gaps and other opportunities, coping with crises, solving problems, and applying knowledge in many other ways comprise a core of functional actions within successful organizations. Achieving those diverse but integrated activities requires a spirit of enterprise uniting people to achieve the organization's objectives and to endure the demanded sacrifices.

The five necessary conditions will not compensate for each other. If an enterprise lacks up-to-date knowledge, it may fail as a result of bad decisions. Even the most sophisticated knowledge provides no benefit without useful applications. If people are not inspired by a company's objectives, internal conflicts may create severe inefficiencies. Lacking a constructive vision of the future results in short-lived success. Progressive competitors will soon cast the future to fit their plans.

The conditions of success do not happen automatically. A catalytic presence of able management forms them. Management, the fifth success factor, is ultimately responsible for introducing and maintaining the other four. Management consequently requires skill in both social, interpersonal relationships and in the use of technical tools. That job description is demanding.

L-M theory provides the logic for integrating judgmental linguistic information with the qualitative and quantitative numerical information being processed in organizations. That information carries the signals of technological change as well as functional feedbacks. Systems thinking, hierarchy theory, and LST are used to integrate a battery of methodologies and methods to provide a package of interrelated management procedures. A theory of management observation and communication explains how information from accounting information systems (AIS) and from management information systems (MIS) may be integrated with management reports, procedure manuals, interviews, questionnaires, and so forth to support a participative motivational management style. Thus, it may meet the need for integrative general management.

A PREVIEW

Management observation and communication theory is comprehensive. As such, it provides a way to examine complex questions in detail.

Chapter 2 discusses fundamental elements of LST as they relate to management observation and communication. It explores living systems at the organizational level, giving examples of matter-energy and information processes at that level.

Chapter 3 is a general discussion of L-M theory. It sets L-M theory in the context of general systems theory and explains the fundamental ideas that comprise it. This chapter sets the stage for the rest of the book. The following chapters provide applications of the theory that examine typical communications in organizations in order to discover the concrete processes observed by the communicators.

Chapters 4 and 5 explain how to use L-M theory to construct and use backdrops to analyze organizational communications. Variables and their values, hierarchies, combinational analyses, coexistence, cause-and-effect relationships, and so forth are discussed in considerable depth.

Chapter 6 explains how to combine the results of the analyses of Chapters 4 and 5 to obtain the big picture.

Chapter 7 covers syntactical analysis, including such methods as cognitive networks, syntactic graphs, propositional calculus, and psychologic. These methods emphasize the relationships among terms.

Chapters 8 and 9 discuss semantic analysis, providing illustrations of its use. Several semantic methods are discussed.

Chapter 10 summarizes the main ideas and philosophy of management observation and communication theory.

REFERENCES

Einstein, A. (1961). *Relativity, the special and general theory,* trans. by Robert W. Lawson. New York: Crown Publishers.

Gibbs, J. W. (1902). *Elementary principles of statistical mechanics.* New Haven, Conn.: Yale University Press.

Heiskanen, H. (1975). A systems theoretical approach to the analysis of social actions and decisions. *Annales Academiae Scientiarum Fennicae,* Ser. B. Tom. 191, Helsinki.

Heiskanen, H., and T. Airaksinen. (1979). From subjective welfare to social value: Axiology in methodological and philosophical perspective. *Annales Academiae Scientiarum Fennicae,* Ser. B. Tom. 201, Helsinki.

Hill, A. V. (1931). *Adventures in biophysics.* University of Pennsylvania Press.

Kohler, W. (1921). Die physischen gestalten in Ruhe und in stationaren Zustard. Braunschveig?: Vieweg.

———. (1927). Zuru Problem der Regulation. *Roux's Archiv* 112.

———. (1938). *The place of values in the world of fact.* New York: Liveright.

Miller, J. G. (1978). *Living systems.* McGraw-Hill.

Swanson, G. A., and J. G. Miller. (1989). *Measurement and interpretation in accounting: A living systems theory view.* Westport, Conn.: Greenwood Press.

von Bertalanffy, L. (1950). The theory of open systems and biology. *Science* 3: 23–29.

———. (1956). General systems theory. *Vol. 1. General Systems:* 1–3.

———. (1968). *General Systems Theory.* New York: Braziller.

2

Elements of Living Systems Theory

Management observation and communication theory is composed of certain important elements of L-M theory and LST. This chapter discusses the important elements of LST, and Chapter 3 covers L-M theory.

Both theories are conceptual frameworks. The direct concern of L-M theory is the arrangement of elements of conceptual systems, while LST is directly concerned with concrete systems. LST attempts to define such structures and processes as unambiguously as possible.

Concrete processes should be measured to the extent possible with current measurement technology. They should be assessed through other observation methodologies when measurements cannot be made. LST instructs the actions of measuring and assessing concrete processes.

THE GREAT GULF

Managers introduce the future based on conceptual systems they form in their brains and on interactions among those systems in the human environment. L-M theory interprets conceptual systems and integrates them to form specific abstracted systems (i.e., organizational management theories). It consequently instructs the development of such systems.

Popular management theories have oscillated between top-down (e.g., Drucker 1967) and bottom-up (e.g., Edwards Deming's management method in Walton 1986) approaches. Connecting the top to the bottom and the bottom to the top continues to be a major problem. Situations in which managers merrily believe their organizations are developing in one way while the actual developments are in other directions are not uncommon. Like the rich man and Lazareth of the Bible, a great gulf develops between the manager and the managed. The gap often grows unrecognized until it is too late to bridge. The demise of Eastern Airlines may be the classic example.

Fortunately, large modern Western corporations are mostly robust, and managers, not the managed, are sent to hell. However, that is not always the case, and productive, contributing organizations sometimes disintegrate with attendant human suffering and community turmoil.

Management observation and communication theory encourages and instructs the building of bridges across the grand middle that lies between the measurable concrete processes of human organizations and the very abstract but essential dreams of management for the future. It is not a theory designed to instigate hype for changing directions. That type of theory (e.g., Peters 1987 and Drucker 1969) is a necessary part of an evolving economy. The theory of observation and communication, however, is more basic. It provides the means of determining whether hype theories are working—whether they actually are accomplishing their purposes. Hype theories are more art than science; management observation and communication theory is more science than art. Management advances by refining both its art and its science.

Although the subjects of L-M theory and LST are equally important to managers, this book emphasizes applications of L-M theory. This chapter, consequently, is only an introduction to some far-reaching LST ideas. Although this book does not do it, these ideas can be applied with the same level of detail characteristic of the L-M theory methods introduced throughout the rest of the book.

LIVING SYSTEMS THEORY ORIGINS

The book *Living Systems* by James Grier Miller is the seminal work on LST (1978). LST represents the ideas that emerged over a thirty-year period as a group of prominent scientists developed a general conceptual framework that would extend scientific advances in natural science to biological and social studies (Miller 1953, 1955). Miller states, "We were stimulated to undertake our activities by suggestions from physical scientists, among them Enrico Fermi and Leo Szilard, who felt a heavy responsibility for the fearsome developments in nuclear weapons and who thought that, because we understood so little about why men fight and kill, the development of the sciences of man should be accelerated" (Miller 1978: xv–xvi). Observing that natural sciences had advanced rapidly after general theories were proposed, the physical scientists suggested that the group try a similar strategy.

A general systems theory proposed by von Bertalanffy became the theoretical approach. He defined systems as sets of elements standing in interaction and believed such systems can be specified by families of differential equations (von Bertalanffy 1956). That view was consistent with Alfred Lord Whitehead's philosophy of organisms. He viewed life as composed of organisms made up of lower-level organisms and making up higher-level organisms, all related and interacting in various degrees (Whitehead 1925). Such systems thinking generated a large body of literature and penetrated virtually every discipline, including management, to one extent or another.

MANAGEMENT AND LST

LST identifies a hierarchy of eight levels of life from cells to supranational systems (Table 1.1). The organization level is located between the group and the community levels. Management, as it is commonly perceived, is an activity of the organization level of living systems.

Living systems at the eight levels all have twenty types of critical processes called *subsystems*. Those processes must occur for any living system to survive in earth's environment. The twenty processes are so similar across the eight hierarchical levels of life that they may be considered commonalities.

The processes of every subsystem must occur if a system continues to exist. However, the processes of all subsystems, except the decider subsystem, may be dispersed to other living systems. Only the decider subsystem cannot be dispersed to another system.

Management is the decider subsystem at the organization level. Some kinds of organizations, such as governments, use other terms, such as *administration,* for the decider subsystem. Those statements are idealistic to the extent that every organization has a physically identifiable decider subsystem, but every organization chart does not necessarily identify it. Persons designated as part of management may or may not be elements of the decider subsystem. They are elements of the decider if they in fact decide issues and control the organization.

Management is not the decider to the extent that a gap exists between the conceptual systems of managers describing an organization and the measurable concrete processes of that organization. As the grand middle grows larger, management becomes less and less the decider. As it grows smaller, management and the decider subsystem become more the same.

Management observation and communication theory formalizes the connections between management conceptual systems and concrete processes of organizations, and so builds bridges across the gap. Because its methods are participative, the very action of building bridges narrows the gap.

The position of organizations in the hierarchy of human systems involves managers in controlling the relations and interactions of both organization components (groups and persons with their respective artifacts within organizations) and the organization with its environment (suprasystems such as communities, societies, and supranational systems). As used in LST, the term *controlling* does not imply a process involving only internal aspects.

LST VIEW OF ORGANIZATIONS

A system is any related and interacting set of elements. The universe of all systems is divided into the following three types: concrete systems, which are non-random arrangements of matter, energy, and information transmissions in a region of physical space having components that interact over time; conceptual systems, which are composed of symbols and borne on information markers in the brains of organisms, and abstracted systems, which are similar to conceptual systems except that they are borne on information markers in the human environment.

Concrete systems are divided into two major types, living and nonliving. Nonliving systems exist over definite periods and move from a state of negative entropy (organization) to a state of entropy (random disorganization), according to the second law of thermodynamics. Living systems extend their existence indefinitely by importing highly organized matter, energy and information transmissions, breaking down those elements for repair and growth and exporting less-organized elements.

The entropic condition toward which all relatively closed systems (e.g., the physical element uranium) are progressing is called *steady state* by physical scientists. The extended negative-entropic state of living systems is termed *dynamic steady state, homeostasis,* or *fluxuous steady state* by systems scientists.

Humans are living systems at the organism level. Conceptual systems are formed mainly in human brains. As humans learned to communicate they formed public symbolic systems termed *abstracted systems,* in various environmental media, such as the air, which carries sound waves, and clay tablets, which bear inscriptions. Higher-order human systems are made possible by such symbolic systems and incorporate them as integral parts.

Organizations are higher-order living systems. Such human systems are characterized by the same twenty types of critical processes essential for the continuation of living systems at other hierarchical levels. Examples of organization components that comprise most of those subsystems are given in Table 2.1. Those commonalities across hierarchical levels are explained by the principle of *fray-out,* which asserts that higher levels of living systems emerge as lower-level systems differentiate and specialize their own functions.

Organizations may be totipotential or partipotential. Totipotential organizations perform all twenty critical processes within their own boundaries. Partipotential organizations disperse some critical processes outwardly to other systems—laterally to other organizations or down to groups or persons. All critical subsystems may be dispersed except the decider. Without a decider to control its relationships and interactions, an organization cannot exist.

Typical organizational units such as operations, sales, and accounting are not organized along the lines of the twenty critical subsystems. The principle of fray-

Table 2.1
Components of the 19 Critical Subsystems of an Organization

3.1 SUBSYSTEMS WHICH PROCESS BOTH MATTER-ENERGY AND INFORMATION

3.1.1 Reproducer. Any organization or group that produces an explicit or implicit charter for a new organization; may be downwardly dispersed to a single person.

3.1.2 Boundary. Such subsidiary organizations or groups as guards, doorkeepers, police, personnel offices, admitting officers, admissions committees, membership committees, purchasing departments, personnel at receiving and loading docks, inspectors, receptionists, tour guides, ticket sellers and takers, maintenance staffs, janitorial staffs, military censors, security officers, library committees, loan committees, credit departments, organization officers, and mail-room employees; may be upwardly dispersed to other organizations which serve the entire society; downwardly dispersed to one or all persons in the organization; artifacts such as building, fence, city wall, dike

3.2 SUBSYSTEMS WHICH PROCESS MATTER-ENERGY

3.2.1 Ingestor. Such subsidiary organizations or groups as receiving departments, loading-dock workers, purchasing departments, buyers, selection committees, receptionists, admitting officers, admissions committees, orientation groups, missionaries, guides, porters, recruiters, and doormen; may be downwardly dispersed to particular persons

3.3 SUBSYSTEMS WHICH PROCESS INFORMATION

3.3.1 Input transducer. Such subsidiary organizations or groups as military intelligence agency or unit; guards, lookouts, fire watchers, meteorologists, astronomers, and others who observe and report upon environmental conditions or changes; market research department, persons that report on product or service acceptance or on economic and social trends which may affect the organization; sales department and others that take orders for the organization's products or services; intake department of social service or other organizations; medical personnel who take histories and examine patients on admission to clinics or hospitals; complaint department; legal department that obtains patents or licenses; radar, radio, and telephone operators; library acquisition staff; solicitors of money or credit for an organization; ticket sellers; dues collectors; tax collectors; and bank tellers; may be outwardly dispersed to consultants or researchers from another organization or downwardly dispersed to individual persons who transduce information inputs; artifacts include such communication and detection devices as

(continued)

19

Table 2.1 (Continued)

telescope, field glasses, radar, radio, telephones, television

3.3.2 Internal transducer. Such subsidiary organizations or groups as make reports within an organization or ascertain needs, attitudes, or efficiency of components or subcomponents; spokesmen for components, like committee chairmen, department heads, union stewards and other officials, public opinion pollers, inspectors; bookkeepers, comptroller's office, payroll department, accountants; operations analysts; citizens' groups or organizations; may be outwardly dispersed to union stewards who speak for the union, another organization, or consultants from another organization; or downwardly to individuals who report opinions or activities or start rumors; artifacts such as computer, other business machines, microphone, telephone, closed-circuit television, typewriter, other writing materials, time clock, suggestion box

3.3.3 Channel and net. Such subsidiary organizations or groups as private telephone exchange with switchboard operators, communications maintenance men; messengers,executives, liaison officers, department heads, supervisors, officers of citizens' groups, heads of households, secretaries; may be upwardly dispersed to communications personnel of the society, including employees of telephone and telegraph companies, the postal service, messenger services, broadcasting services, newspapers and other publications; or downwardly to individual employees, voters, or other persons; artifacts such as letter papers, electronic channel and related equipment, vehicle that distributes publications, armored car that carries money and securities, computer

3.2.2 Distributor. Such subsidiary organizations or groups as operate organizational transportation facilities such as traffic bureau and police; supply officers; drivers; helicopter or airplane pilots; train engineers in mine; elevator operators; waiters, busboys, ushers; car, truck, and bus drivers; quartermaster department of army; may be upwardly dispersed to the society, as when national railroad carries freight between company plants or when a supranational pipeline, railroad, steamship, or airline does so; or downwardly, as when people walk or drive their own cars; animals such as donkeys and horses; artifacts such as road, trail, passageway; bus, subway, train, truck, moving sidewalk, escalator, stair, fire escape, elevator, conveyor belt, chute, pipeline, pneumatic tube, dumbwaiter; traffic control system, service facility, check-out counter, and toll booth; tray, plate, bucket, cup

20

3.2 SUBSYSTEMS WHICH PROCESS MATTER-ENERGY

3.2.3 Converter. Such subsidiary organizations or groups as operate electric generating plants, oil refineries, steel mills, glass factories, packing plants, canneries, flour mills, dairies, many chemical plants, textile mills; may be upwardly dispersed to the society, as when an aluminum factory converts ore metal for an entire nation; artifacts such as knife, axe, hammer, refining equipment, ore-conversion machinery, cotton gin, threshing machine, grinder, chopper, melter, crusher

3.2.4 Producer. Such subsidiary organizations or groups as production workers in factories, cooks, bakers, binders; maintenance workers, health personnel; artifacts such as manufacturing machine, tool, assembly line, maintenance equipment, medical instruments, and drugs

3.2.5 Matter-energy storage. Such subsidiary organizations or groups as factory personnel in charge of supplies; personnel in charge of warehouse, garage, parking area, reservoir, stockroom, cattle pen, storage tank, grain elevator, coatroom, waiting room, dock, holding area, airport airway; supply clerks; may be laterally dispersed to departments of an organization; or downwardly to individual persons in it; artifacts like parking lot, barn, silo, warehouse, storage room, closet, file, container

3.3 SUBSYSTEMS WHICH PROCESS INFORMATION

3.3.4 Decoder. Such subsidiary organizations or groups as foreign-language translators, cryptographers, signal officers, telegraphers, radar and sonar operators, experts in reporting technical and scientific findings; persons who use confidential business codes; religious leaders and mystics; meteorologists and other interpreters of signs; may be upwardly dispersed to society, like diplomats who translate documents for companies in their countries; or downwardly to individual members and employees; artifacts such as teletypewriter, print reader, computer; other data processing machines, pattern-recognition machines like check readers and punched-card readers

3.3.5 Associator. No system at this level has an associator subsystem; this subsystem is downwardly dispersed to individual persons or, occasionally, outwardly dispersed to operations researchers or management consultants from another organization; an artifact such as a computer may do some associating for an organization

3.3.6 Memory. Such subsidiary organizations or groups as filing department, bookkeeping department, secretaries, computer experts, bibliographers, librarians, curators; may be upwardly dispersed to banks, stockbrokers, libraries; or downwardly dispersed to individual secretaries and specialists; artifacts such as paper, book, film, microfilm, magnetic tape, computer memory, filing cabinet, container, teaching machine

3.3.7 Decider. Such subsidiary organizations or groups as board of directors, executives, judges, rabbis, bishops, commanders, captains, stockholders, members, voters; may be upwardly dispersed to court-appointed officials; outwardly dispersed to management firms; laterally dispersed to component

(continued)

Table 2.1 (Continued)

3.2.6 Extruder. Such subsidiary organizations or groups as city department of sanitation, street cleaning, and sewers; personnel that operate garbage, trash, express, and delivery trucks; bus, train, boat, and plane crews; packing or shipping department; police or others empowered to expel intruders from organization or its territory; discipline committee that discharges or expels employees or members; personnel officers; janitors, custodians, maids, cleaning staff; doctors and nurses who participate in discharge of patients from hospitals; college officials who graduate students; may be outwardly dispersed to city sanitation department that removes wastes from organization territory; laterally to families in a community where each family disposes of its own wastes; or downwardly when each person disposes of his own wastes; artifacts such as dump truck, other vehicle, barge, sewer pipe, smokestack, waste can, mop, broom, street-cleaning equipment, dolly, chute, conveyor belt, firearm

3.2.7 MOTOR. Such subsidiary organizations or groups as domesticated animals; crew, pilots, drivers, operators, or maintenance personnel of man-animal or man-machine systems; may be downwardly dispersed to individual persons in an organization, as when an army marches; or upwardly dispersed to transportation operated for the entire society, such as airline, steamship line, railroad, bus line, trucking line; artifacts such as ship, aircraft, spacecraft, truck, bus; tool or machine such as earthmover, tractor, saw, shovel

3.2.8 Supporter. No living supporter known at this level, but organizations must make use of parcels of land or artifacts such as building, platform, ship, road, vehicle

groups; downwardly dispersed to a single ruler or executive; artifacts such as computer

3.3.8 Encoder. Such subsidiary organizations or groups as write and edit speeches, publications, other communications; code communications; translate languages; design trademarks, buildings, other artifacts; act as lawyers, labor relations experts, lobbyists; advertising or public relations department; may be joint with decider, output transducer subsystems; outwardly dispersed to organizations like advertising, public relations firms, or trade association; downwardly to individual persons acting in above capacities, salesperson, recruiter, solicitor; artifacts such as writing materials, paints, computer

3.3.9 Output transducer. Such subsidiary organizations groups as public relations department; spokesmen; labor negotiators; salespeople; missionaries; lobbyists and pressure groups; secretaries; publication, mailing, or circulation department; printers; actors and other performers; media department; broadcasters; maintenance staff for electronic equipment; may be joint with decider or encoder components; outwardly dispersed to other organizations like advertising agency or television station; downwardly dispersed to decentralized groups or individual persons; artifacts such as electronic answering device, public address system, television, radio; printing, duplicating, and mailing equipment; computer

Source: James Grier Miller, Living Systems, McGraw-Hill, 1978, pp. 606-607

out also explains why that is the case. Differentiation and specialization occur by arranging the critical processes in different clusters, often dividing a particular process among two or more organizational units. As organizations grow larger, organizational units also attempt to develop their own critical subsystems, thus becoming more totipotential and less directly dependent on the organization for their processes.

The twenty critical concrete subsystems of organizations process various forms of matter, energy, and information transmissions, such as buildings and inventory, electricity, and telephone messages. They do this by importing and exporting the various forms at different rates. Actually, organizations may be viewed totally as processes, as changes over time. An illusion of unchanging form, however, is produced by the rate differentials of subprocesses. A building, for example, remains in process much longer than an inventory and is used to store it. People ordinarily call the illusion formed by more enduring processes *structures* and identify the more rapid import-export flows with the term *processes*.

Unfortunately, the possible variations of process rates form a continuum, not a discrete scale, and certainly do not fall neatly into two categories. Although the ordinary notion of structure has great common-sense appeal, it is not very useful for measurements because the location of the line dividing process and structure is completely arbitrary.

Swanson and Miller (1989: 59, 99) give the term *structure* a different meaning. To them, structure is the location of the concrete elements of organizations in an instant. That, of course, is itself a fiction. Concrete systems simply cannot exist outside of time. Their structures continually are being changed by process over time. Nevertheless, a structure thus defined can be calculated by observing the imports and exports across an organization's boundary in a certain period, and by subtracting one from the other to determine the structure at the instant marking the end of the period. Iterations of that algorithm can map the continuing existence of an organization.

Although it may be popular at times to emphasize chaos, uncertainty, and fuzzy boundaries, none of those things make organizations. Relations and interactions make organizations. Although it is important to recognize that the interactions of concern to human systems fluctuate within ranges that themselves fluctuate over time, it is also important to realize that those ranges are relatively narrow.

Defining structure as the three-dimensional arrangement of concrete system elements outside of time provides a means of segmenting the fuzzy, chaotic, uncertain processes of organizations into observable units on the time dimension. Such units are not only intuitively observable but may be observed through measurement methodology as well.

The term *process* is defined as all change over time in the concrete elements of an organization. Structure and process together form its *state*. Describing the state of an organization requires descriptions of both the processes over a certain period and the structures at the instances marking the beginning and ending of that period. Processes are observed by measuring the inflows and outflows occurring in the period at the boundary of the organization. Structures are calculated as the residuals of previous process measurements.

Types of processes may be divided usefully into two categories: *Functions* are readily reversible actions that change structure from moment to moment. *Histories* are less readily reversible actions that change both structure and function. Functions are processes of the first degree, and histories are processes of the second degree. Technological advances and authoritative changes cause histories.

Organizations have *purposes*, which are internal, and *goals*, which are external. All organizations develop a preferential hierarchy of values of interrelationships and interactions among their components. Decision rules emerge from the preferential hierarchy that determines an organization's preference for a particular steady state, which is the organization's fundamental purpose. The complex of values that is compared to information entering the organization determines how that information is associated and how any related matter-energy elements are distributed. Such a fundamental purpose may be subdivided into multiple and simultaneous purposes.

Organizations also may have external goals that are pursued to satisfy their purposes. Organizations are formed in mature societies to perform societal and community subsystem processes. In such an environment, the goals of organizations are constrained by the purposes of societies and communities. If that were not the case, society and community orders of human systems would not exist.

In summary, the LST view of organizations is a systemic view. It views all existence from the living systems perspective. From that perspective organizations are concrete living systems—higher-order human systems composed of identifiable subsystems and components. Those higher-order human systems incorporate various forms of matter-energy, such as materials, people, electricity, and information transmissions.

A GRAND VIEW OF MANAGEMENT

Modern human history can be viewed as an attempt to evolve higher-order human systems beyond the organization level. When societies remove the independent existence—the purpose—of organizations, societies themselves collapse into organizations controlled by a central multiechelon decider subsystem. To continue to exist, societies must maintain the relative independence of the organizations that comprise them while constraining any one organization's power to control. The societal decider subsystem should be distributed widely among a society's various components. Pluralistic societies are advancements, but simply separating political, economic, and military components does not ensure that such components will not collapse into organizations powerful enough to invade the control of others.

The advancement of civilization depends more on scientific advances in the management of organizations than most people realize. Managers should recognize that while gaining control of more and more resources is in fact how organizations survive, the survival of societies depends on sufficiently constraining the accumulation of such control. That statement does not refer to governments constraining businesses. Governments are organizations as are businesses, banks, and stock and commodity exchanges. Societal constraint should be exercised by relationships and interactions among all organizations in society, forming negative feedbacks that maintain society in a dynamic steady state (Swanson and Marsh 1991).

Goals of societies depend on their degree of potentiality. Totipotential societies do not necessarily have goals. Partipotential societies must pursue goals to disperse outwardly the critical processes they cannot perform within their own boundaries. Pursuing different external goals to satisfy internal purposes can introduce positive feedbacks that change the dynamic steady states of societies.

As a consequence of that action, managing organizations within partipotential societies requires more environmental management (interactions among organizations) than totipotential societies do. Maintaining societal dynamic steady states in totipotential societies already requires an intense environmental management effort.

How do organizational managers strive to increase their control of resources while simultaneously constraining that effort? That is the grand question humans are just now learning to answer. If the answer is learned, a new day may dawn for humankind. Ignoring the question as though organizations may be managed without regard to their environments likely will continue the cycles of political dictatorships, economic despots, military conquests, and booms and busts for the average person.

MANAGEMENT INFORMATION

Information in concrete systems is defined as the arrangement (patterns) of their elements at an instant and the order (patterns) of the elements over time. Managing concrete processes requires that such information be reduced spatially and transmitted to the spatiotemporal proximity of the manager. Reduced information is borne on relatively small amounts of matter-energy called *information markers*. LST identifies twelve critical information processing subsystems, including the decider (manager). The other eleven subsystems process information to and from the decider, enabling the decider to manage the system.

The information processing subsystems all perform particular vital functions for reducing, storing, and transmitting information in earth's environment. The *reproducer* provides information capable of giving rise to new similar organizations. The *boundary* excludes information markers from an organization or permits their entry. Information markers are brought into the system by the *input transducer*. The *internal transducer* moves information markers among organization components over the *channel and net* (the physical routes for information flows). The code of environmental information is altered by the *decoder* to one understood within the organization. The *associator* forms enduring associations among the information in the organization, while the *memory* stores information in the organization for various periods. The *timer* provides information from the original template and the environment for sequencing processes. The *encoder* alters the private code of organizational information to one understood in the environment, and the *output transducer* changes information markers used inside the organization to forms that can be transmitted in the organization's environment.

All these activities are necessary for physically processing information about the concrete operations of organizations. They are also involved with hypothetical ideas, if those ideas are transmitted among persons in an organization and in its environment. LST is concerned with the physical processes of reducing and storing concrete system information and transmitting it to managers. L-M theory is concerned with reducing (abstracting) concrete system information and connecting that reduced information to abstracted systems that incorporate hypothetical ideas of managers (management theories and stated goals of organizations).

Management information is, in the final analysis, concerned with the matter-energy processes of organizations—people, machines, energy, and so on. Such processes are the fundamental essence of organizations. LST identifies ten critical matter-energy processing subsystems.

Each matter-energy subsystem performs a function vital to the survival of living systems on earth. The reproducer processes matter-energy forms that give rise to other similar organizations. The boundary excludes certain forms of matter-energy while holding the organization components together. The *ingestor* moves matter-energy forms across the boundary into the organization and the *extruder* moves such forms out. The *distributor* moves such forms around within the organization, and the *motor* moves the organization or parts of it in its environment. The *converter* changes forms of matter-energy brought into the organization into more useful forms for the other matter-energy processes of the organization. The *producer* forms stable associations of different matter-energy forms that endure over extended periods. *Matter-energy storage* retains matter-energy forms in the organization for different periods, and the *supporter* maintains the proper spatial relationships among organizational units.

Information-processing subsystems process information about all of the critical matter-energy processing subsystems and the organization's environment. They also process information about their own processes and structures, because they themselves are composed of matter-energy forms, such as people, machines, and energy.

MEASUREMENT

The concrete processes of organizations theoretically are all measurable. They are not measurable to the extent that measurement theory and technology have not advanced far enough.

Measurement is a particular way of observing—abstracting information about—physical objects. It has two aspects: comparing an object to a scale or standard and assigning quantitative values to the objects. The first aspect requires identifying the most fundamental elements of a system under investigation and observing those elements by placing close to them information markers that bear the scale or standard and comparing the two. Measurement makes it possible for two independent observers to describe the same object in the same way with relatively little error.

Measurement is important because different people perceive the same object differently. Scales are constructed by people, and, consequently, the relationships among a scale's elements are publicly understood. By agreeing to observe objects with direct reference to scales, individual biases in determining what exists can be minimized.

People investigate concrete processes for some reason, for example, to determine whether an organization was more successful this period than last or to assess the performance of an organizational unit manager. Those reasons typically are generalizations of very complex interactions among many variables on many different dimensions. How measurements of the many variables relate to the global reason for an investigation is the interpretation of the measurements.

Measurements and interpretations are validated on different bases and thus should be clearly distinguished from each other. Measurements are validated on empirical evidence. Interpretations are validated by the consensus of a group. If managers bypass measuring concrete processes by broadly intuiting organizational conditions, the reason for collecting organizational information can easily bias the interpretation of those conditions. Measurement, to the contrary, increases the difficulty of biasing the information and increases the influence of what actually exists.

Some managers insist that they do not want to be overly influenced by the difficulty of a chosen course of action. However, whether a particular bit of management information constitutes a negative or positive feedback, its utility to the organization depends upon its objective, valid, and reliable description of the integrity of some part of the organization or upon its environment, and not upon its feed effect. To assert that management may be deterred from some ultimate goal if present conditions are known and therefore should not discover them denies the information's usefulness. Although war stories often venerate ignorance, long-term success depends upon identifying and reducing important information, not upon whimsical ignorance.

Organizations are composed of many different forms of matter-energy. Important management information is obtained by observing different forms on a common attribute (e.g., different land parcels on the attribute area, and different apples on the attribute size). Measurement scales are introduced to accomplish this. Scales and attributes are connected. A particular scale is a quantified abstracted system borne on information markers that may be used to abstract information by comparing it to different forms and assigning its values to those forms (e.g., number of acres to land on the attribute area, and number of bushels to apples on the attribute size).

Managers observe organizations through many different scales for many different purposes on many different attributes. The extent to which an entire organization may be viewed as a whole depends on the extent to which an attribute is common to all organizational elements.

A unique contribution of modern accounting systems to management information is that they make it possible for managers to view organizations as organic wholes. Those systems observe the inflows and outflows of different matter-energy forms on an attribute common to all. That attribute is specific exchange value, and it is measured in monetary units comprising a ratio scale.

The observation methodology of accounting systems is very robust. It uses a double-entry method that records both the inflow and outflow transaction of every exchange at an organization's boundary. That method comprehensively maps certain actual matter-energy and information transmission flows of organizations. The methodology arises from the most fundamental process of market-based economies—the exchange. In market economies, reciprocating transactions are motivated by each other to form exchanges. Modern accounting systems observe those transactions with a coupled double entry.

All the concrete processes of organizations can be viewed together on the attribute specific exchange value in terms of the monetary scale. No other attribute and scale can provide that comprehensive view.

SUMMARY

This chapter describes organizations as concrete observable systems, a fundamental view expounded in detail by LST. Our theory of management observation and communication incorporates the physical, concrete view of organizations. The following chapters discuss how managers may use L-M theory to discover

observations of concrete processes in the communications among people and
machines in organizations, and to connect the information about those observations to the theories and goals of management.

REFERENCES

Drucker, P. F. (1969). *The age of discontinuity*. New York: Harper and Row.
———. (1967). *The effective executive*. New York: Harper and Row.
Miller, J. G. (1978). *Living systems*. New York: McGraw-Hill.
———. (1953). Introduction. In *Symposium: Profits and problems of homeostatic models
in the behavioral sciences,* ed. Members of the Committee on Behavioral Sciences,
University of Chicago, 1–11. Chicago Behavioral Sciences Publications no. 1.
———. (1955). Toward a general theory for the behavioral sciences. *American Psycholo-
gy* 10: 513–31.
Peters, T. (1987). *Thriving on chaos*. New York: Harper and Row.
Swanson, G. A., and H. L. Marsh. (1991). *Internal auditing theory: A systems view*.
Westport, Conn.: Greenwood Press.
Swanson, G. A., and J. G. Miller. (1989). *Measurement and interpretation in accounting:
A living systems theory view*. Westport, Conn.: Greenwood Press.
von Bertalanffy, L. (1956). General systems theory. *General Systems*. 1: 1–7.
Walton, M. (1986). *The deming management method*. New York: Petnam Publishing
Group.
Whitehead, A. N. (1925). *Science and the modern world*. New York: Macmillan.

3

Elements of Linguistic-Mathematical Theory

Chapter 1 introduced the idea of systems and suggested that simple but nontrivial notion could be used extensively to simplify managers' perceptions of the complex organizations they control. A system is any set of related and interacting elements. Because the elements, relationships, and interactions may be very different from system to system, virtually all matters of interest to humans may be viewed as systems and thus studied in a common manner.

Chapter 2 overviewed some important elements of LST. The living systems view of organizations is assumed throughout the rest of the book. This chapter clarifies the idea of general systems theory and sketches the fundamental systems concepts mentioned in Chapter 1. It is essentially a broad overview of L-M theory. L-M theory concerns arranging organizational information. Management observation and communication theory views organizations from the perspective of LST. L-M theory arranges organizational information to manage the concrete processes of organizations according to the perspective of LST.

GENERAL SYSTEMS THEORY

More than forty years ago von Bertalanffy (1950) was concerned about the unity of science and called for a superstructure applicable in various scientific fields. He suggested that a general systems theory would be the requisite tool in the search for a uniform conceptual construct as it is suitable for diverse disciplines, and that the theory would thus extend beyond the conventional departments of science.

Now, after more than four decades, the basic situation hardly has changed. On the one hand, the body of knowledge in the social sciences has increased essentially in the interval, but it still consists of causal and atomistic minor theories.

On the other hand, interest in systems thinking has increased, producing many remarkable works on the subject, such as Miller's living systems (1978) and Klir's architecture of problem solving (1985). Nevertheless, many obstacles remain both in the social sciences and in systems research. Troncale lists urgent goals in systems research as: producing a consensus glossary in systems science, synthesizing findings in the literature, demonstrating isomorphies across disciplines, counterbalancing the trend toward fragmentation, developing tools for the operationalization of systems, coupling research with the application of theories and databases, and developing a specific methodology for systems research (1985).

A partial answer to these problems lies in L-M theory. We have focused it on management because management by necessity integrates the knowledge of various natural and social sciences. The same theory may be used to integrate entire disciplines.

Such a general systems theory is a collection of principles according to which observations, research, and literature findings can be divided into elements and combined into compilations for further statistical, mathematical, computational, or other treatment. Those actions will form wiser theories, find isomorphies, produce practicable applications, and serve other purposes for which science is intended besides the topic at hand. A functioning general systems theory that fulfills these specifications provides a solution to most of the goals set by von Bertalanffy.

EXPECTATIONS OF A GENERAL SYSTEMS THEORY

To be usefully applied to organizational problems a general systems theory should have certain basic characteristics. Listed here are the most important ones:

1. *Freedom from concrete substance.* A general systems theory provides only the principles according to which information about observations is divided and combined, without any reference to observational, concrete data other than examples. It should be as substance-free as algebra or geometry. Very few of the general systems theories available, however, are entirely free from real theory substance in this sense. At least, they operate with real theory concepts such as learning, evolution, and so forth, or they examine information or energy flow instead of examining changes, influence, relations, or other "empty" concepts.

2. *Explicitness.* To qualify as a scientifically disciplined method, a general systems theory ought to be expressed exactly and explicitly. This is seldom the case. Most general theories are expressed vaguely, making their applications by anyone but their inventors very difficult or even impossible.

3. *Parsimony.* Systems theories sometimes contain too many concepts to be economical. This is partly due to the introduction of concepts belonging to a

communications vocabulary itself. When data is classified by its own charac-teristics instead of being divided into entities, variables, or values, the volume of classifications may become overwhelming.

4. *Freedom from value loadings.* Some general systems theories not only contain real theoretical data but also tend to influence and change the concrete world in accordance with some social philosophy. They are not content merely to make the common sensical more precise, accurate, and logical. Such systems theories include, for example, the Marxist and other so-called critical systems theories.

5. *Instrumentality.* A general systems theory should serve research as a neu-tral tool. The instrumentality of general systems theories should be jealously protected, and such theories should be prevented from becoming ends in them-selves.

BASIC IDEAS OF L-M THEORY

A general systems theory, as defined in the previous section, may be viewed as a collection of ideas used to divide and combine information about observa-tions. Managers succeed or fail depending upon their expertise in sorting infor-mation about organizational processes. L-M theory examines organizational in-formation in the context of the hierarchy of ideas described in Figure 3.1.

Concepts are conceived in the mind and may be used to describe observations. Although all concepts originate that way, L-M theory makes a clear and funda-mental distinction between examining the concepts of a communications vocabu-lary and forming a frame of reference for an examination with a set of theoretical concepts. The most general classification of concepts therefore is divided into the subclassifications *basic concepts* and *auxiliary concepts*. Basic concepts are integral parts of a communications vocabulary being examined. Auxiliary con-cepts are theoretical concepts that refer to basic concepts.

Basic concepts are divided into *terms* and *relations*. Terms have separate and distinct existences, and relations are connections between terms. Terms consist of three elementary types—values, variables, and entities—that are hier-archically related. Collectively exhaustive sets of mutually exclusive values are called *variables*. *Entities* are affairs described by one or more variables. *Values* are organized by relations into variables that, in turn, are organized into an entity, forming an *elementary hierarchy*.

Managers ultimately are concerned with concrete physical systems. The ques-tion of paramount importance is: How are the basic concepts of a communica-tions vocabulary connected to the physical systems? How it is answered deter-mines the degree of control managers can exercise over their organizations. A basic concept may be a holistic description ambiguously referencing multiple,

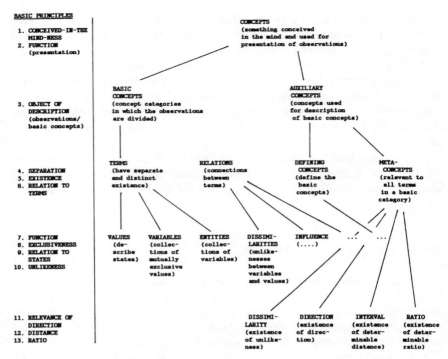

Figure 3.1
Systems Theory Ideas as a Hierarchy

potentially identifiable elements of a physical system, or it may reference only one primitive, basic element at a time. The most basic element of an observed physical system is called a state. The basic concepts of a communications vocabulary should be connected to the physical system it describes by connecting values to states. That connection is called *observation* and is instructed by measurement and assessment theories. The logico-mathematical relationships of L-M theory are important ideas identified in those theories.

Values, variables, and entities clearly are elements of the conceptual systems introduced by people in organizations to describe the processes that concern them. States are the concrete elements they are describing. The terms state and value commonly are used synonomously. We distinguish between concrete and conceptual systems when referring to organizational communications.

Basic concepts together with physical coordinates in space and time comprise the *backdrop* of an observation (Klir 1985: 35). They are the means of describing an observation. Managers, therefore, are concerned directly with basic concepts. L-M theory provides the conceptual framework and procedures for constructing backdrops from particular observations, and for using such backdrops to examine the processes of organizations.

The terms *relations, terms, entities,* and even *basic concepts* and *auxiliary concepts,* are examples of auxiliary concepts. They are part of a theoretical vocabulary introduced to examine the communications language of organizations. A theoretical vocabulary that is separate from a communications vocabulary is, however, not the only set of auxiliary concepts. Concepts of the communications vocabulary also can be auxiliary concepts.

A major theme of management observation and communication theory is that the measurements and assessments of organizational concrete processes can be connected formally to statements of internal purposes and external goals. Such purposes and goals commonly are stated quite abstractly and are connected only intuitively to the measurements and assessments of the physical processes that fundamentally constitute organizations.

L-M theory is used in concrete process management to formalize the connection between measurements and assessments and purposes and goals by augmenting the theoretical vocabulary (the general systems aspect of auxiliary concepts) with the concepts of the communications vocabulary themselves. That arrangement makes it possible to define the terms, relations, and entities—the basic concepts—of the communications vocabulary with reference to the communications vocabulary itself. Consequently, a particular communications concept may be a basic concept in one use and an auxiliary concept in another. Theoretical concepts and communications concepts thus comprise auxiliary concepts. Both types of auxiliary concepts, however, have the same function in L-M theory. For that reason, the distinction between theoretical and communications concepts in auxiliary concepts is not included in Figure 3.1.

The distinction made in Figure 3.1 is between defining concepts, which are used to define other concepts, and metaconcepts, which are relevant to those other concepts. The defining terms and relations of a communications vocabulary (used as variables to define other terms and relations) are called *semantic components.* Any formal connection constructed between measurements and assessments and purposes and goals are only as strong as their definitional components are unambiguous. Consequently, two chapters are devoted to the semantic aspects of L-M theory.

The most common metaconcepts are: existence of unlikeness, existence of direction, existence of determinable distance, and existence of determinable ratio. All four are relevant to states and values, variables, dissimilarities, and influence relations. For example, they classify variables into nominal, ordinal, interval, and ratio variables. Each basic term and relation category has its own specific metaconcepts.

All of those ideas are placed in perspective in Figure 3.2. The term *state* is defined as the actual, stand-alone, most basic element of a system being ob-

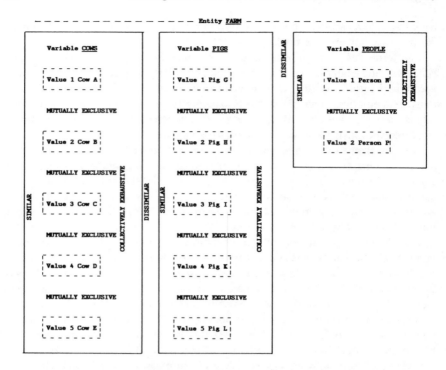

Beginning inside the diagram and working out, the values describe states that are qualified as a variable by the relational metaconcepts "MUTUALLY EXCLUSIVE," "COLLECTIVELY EXHAUSTIVE," and "SIMILAR." The variables are distinguished from each other by the relational metaconcept "DISSIMILAR." Together, the values and variables in hierarchical arrangement constitute the "Entity."

Figure 3.2
Basic Ideas of L-M Theory

served. If the system being observed is a variable, its state is described by a value of that variable. The state of an entity—a higher-order system—is described by the combined value of the entity's variables. It consequently includes relations as well as variable states. As concrete systems advance through hierarchical levels, their states—the most fundamental stand-alone elements—include more and more relations and interactions (subsystems), thereby increasing their physical complexity. Even though the states of higher-order systems can be analyzed physically with terms and relations into the more basic elements of subsystems (reduced), such analyses are not of the higher-order system. That kind of analysis is of the lower-order systems contained in the higher-order one.

The synonymous use of the terms *state* and *value* does not distinguish between the stand-alone object in an observed system and its description in the conceptual or abstracted system of an observer. Mostly, value is used to describe the state of a variable, and state is used to describe the states of entities. The distinction we make is useful for empirical science and the management of concrete processes.

L-M THEORY WAY OF THINKING SUMMARIZED

The point of departure in constructing these ideas is the concept of state. Those stand-alone fundamental elements are related by metaconcepts such as mutual exclusiveness. Different states are mutually exclusive, or they can exist congruently or simultaneously, or both. Different states existing congruently cannot be observed individually. From an observational information point of view, therefore, congruent different states collapse into a single undifferentiated state. Mutually exclusive states, alternatively, can be observed. Different simultaneous states may be observed, if the measurement instrument is precise enough to make them mutually exclusive states.

By means of these metaconcepts we derive the concept of variable, which is a description of a set of possible states—a set of mutually exclusive values. Every value of a variable may describe a state, and the values of all its variables combine to describe the state of an entity.

Two states are relatively unlike or similar to each other. The unlikeness (different values) of mutually exclusive states with regard to a relevant variable is a dissimilarity. Dissimilarities may include further metaconcepts, such as the direction of unlikeness. Subconcepts, such as the nominal, ordinal, interval, and ratio variables, are derived from such metaconcepts. Those level-of-quantification type relations describe connections between states when states are observed in pairs. The connection between two variable states ordinarily is called the *element relation*. Another example of a metavariable (metaconcept) is the purpose for which the pairs are examined—whether one partner is defined or influenced by the other. Each state exists or is examined for a limited period. A state may be simultaneously described as a value of a variable and also as a part of the condition of an identifiable entity forming the entity state.

BACKDROP

Each observation about a state (S_1) is unique. The uniqueness is specified by means of the instant in time (t_1), the identity of the entity (E_1), and the variable (p^1), that is,

$$p^1 \, E_1 \, t_1 = S_1.$$

This is the smallest piece of information described by L-M theory. It reads: the variable p^1 has, by the entity individual E_1 at time t_1, the state S_1. The identity of the entity E_1, the point of time t_1, and often also the variable p^1, are together termed the *backdrop* of the observational information.

The idea of backdrop is important in L-M theory. Chapter 4 is devoted to procedures for constructing backdrops. Although terms and relationships are both important for constructing and using backdrops, constructing backdrops focuses on terms, and using backdrops focuses on relations. Chapter 5 develops procedures for using backdrops.

GENERALITY

Many other concepts relevant to social research and management decisions are derived from metaconcepts. The concept of generality provides an example of this process. Consider an observation in which variable y depends on variable x according to the equation

$$y = a + bx.$$

This observation raises the following questions concerning its backdrop:

1. Is this equation always valid, or only valid during research? This is a question of time generality. If the observation is time-general, it holds good for all instances of time (t_v). If it only holds good during the research process (t_1), it is not time-general but time-specific.
2. For which conditions (states) does it hold good? What is its condition generality? Is it valid only when another variable p^3 has a particular value? Is it valid at all the values of p^3? Is it valid at all values of all variables not in the equation?

In this way, the concepts of generality are derived from the concept of backdrop, and all the concepts of L-M theory are related to the concept of state.

HIERARCHY OF THEORIES

A theoretical frame of reference should comprise several schemes at different levels of abstraction. Such an arrangement is a hierarchy. Figure 3.3 demonstrates the hierarchical characteristics of theories.

At the top are the most abstract systems theories, such as GST and L-M theory. They are free of any references to concrete substance or observational material, meaning that they examine acts and episodes, for example, in terms of entities and other systems theory concepts. They are therefore applicable to the whole range of phenomena. They are completely defined with reference to their own elements.

SEMANTIC DIMENSIONS

ALL PHENOMENA—CONCRETE, CONCEPTUAL, AND ABSTRACTED SYSTEMS	HIERARCHIC LEVEL OF THEORIES	SYSTEMS THEORY CONCEPT CATEGORY	PERFORMER (PERFORMED BY ...)	KIND OF LIVING AGENT	VIEWPOINT (FROM THE VP OF ...)	VIEWPOINT	KIND OF WELFARE AS A MOTIVATOR	KIND OF PERFORMANCE REWARDER
ALL PHENOMENA	GENERAL SYSTEMS THEORY EG. LINGUISTIC-MATHEMATIC THEORY	AN ACT AS AN ENTITY						
LIVING REAL WORLD	LIVING SYSTEMS THEORY	AN ACT AS AN ENTITY	LIVING AGENT					
HUMAN BEHAVIOR	BEHAVIORAL GRAND SOCIAL THEORY	AN ACT AS AN ENTITY	LIVING AGENT	HUMAN				
SOCIAL INTERACTION	THEORY OF DISTRIBUTIVE JUSTICE	AN ACT AS AN ENTITY	LIVING AGENT	HUMAN	DISTRI-BUTION OF WELFARE			
MOTIVATION	THEORY OF MOTIVATION	AN ACT AS AN ENTITY	LIVING AGENT	HUMAN	DISTRI-BUTION OF WELFARE	MOTIVATION		
LEADERSHIP	THEORY OF LEADER'S ESTEEM	AN ACT AS AN ENTITY	LIVING AGENT	HUMAN	DISTRI-BUTION OF WELFARE	MOTIVATION	ESTEEM	
PAY AS A MEANS OF	THEORY OF WAGES (PAY) AS A MOTIVATOR	AN ACT AS AN ENTITY	LIVING AGENT	HUMAN	DISTRI-BUTION OF WELFARE	MOTIVATION	ESTEEM	PAY

NEGLECTED

Figure 3.3
Theories in the Form of a Hierarchy

39

At the next level, systems theories depend on references to concrete substance, but only to the extent that they are applicable to the whole range of elements composing such substance (e.g., living systems). For example, they examine an act not only as an entity but as one performed by a living agent. An example of this kind of systems theory is LST. It is narrower than general systems theory inasmuch as it imposes a particular empirical perspective.

If more real substance constraints are added to the theory of living systems, a grand behavioral theory that examines the behavior of human beings may be obtained. It de-emphasizes other aspects of living systems and emphasizes human behavior.

As more real substance constraints are added, more specific theories are obtained. A theory of distributive justice not only examines acts performed by human beings, but examines them from the viewpoint of distribution of welfare. It thus concentrates on social interaction and neglects other areas of human behavior. Theories of motivation examine only the motivational part of welfare distribution (i.e., welfare in the form of rewards and punishments to influence and guide the behavior of people). Some of the leadership theories examine the esteem of a leader as a means of leading followers. They view leadership from the perspective that followers reward leaders by subordination and punish them by insubordination according to how the leader leads them and behaves personally. That is, the followers try to motivate their leader by their behavior. Wage theories examine, among other things, the extent to which pay and pay systems influence the working morale of wage earners (i.e., how a leader can motivate followers with pay).

LOGICO-MATHEMATICAL NATURE OF BASIC CONCEPTS

Managers are significant consumers of information. Their work essentially is based on it. Managers gather information in a manner similar to that of social scientists. However, they typically gather much more information—so much more that it is often difficult to comprehend. Information simplification, consequently, is an important aspect of management information processes (both accounting information systems and management information systems).

Accounting information systems are fundamentally information communications systems. They measure the concrete processes of organizations, transmit that information to managers and other deciders, and transmit information from deciders to the entire organization. Accounting information is objective in the sense of the term *objective numbering* (Swanson and Miller 1989: 37–53). Accounting's quantifications are not purely abstract. They cannot be divorced from their empirical content. Three bushels of apples added to four bushels of pears do not necessarily get seven generic bushels. In some circumstances, they may be combined as seven bushels of fruit, but that combination has little meaning in other situations.

Management information systems typically focus on decision models. What information, concrete and otherwise, is needed for a particular decision or series of decisions? They seek out limited particular information in a manner very similar to that of scientists. They differ from accounting information systems in that they ordinarily concern sample data, while accounting systems normally concern population data. Management information systems are decision-driven, and accounting information systems are measurement-driven.

Managers use conceptual systems of mathematics and statistics and concrete system computers to simplify information. Using those systems in tandem requires that information be amassed in a form compatible with the rules of science and with computational and mathematical methods.

Galtung suggests that social research follow a system of organization by means of three terms (1970). The first of these is the research unit, which refers to persons, events, acts, things, or other items about which information is gathered. This research unit refers to a separate, independent, or self-contained "thing" with a separate and distinct existence in concrete physical or conceptual reality. For managers, research units are individuals among their personnel, their organization and its components, the activities performed, the organization's products, its machinery, and the like. The second concept is a variable referring to a dimension whose variations, dependence, and other properties the investigator wishes to examine. Examples of variables that interest management are: people's names, occupations, and skills; the objectives and results of the firm; the price and quality of the products; and the age and maintenance costs of the machinery. The third category consists of the values that the research units possess or acquire in the variables. These may be, for example, reactions, changes or consequences in the research units produced, or other variables and stimuli. According to Galtung, the main purpose of all social research is to analyze the dependence and influence of relations among values of variables in different, or in the same, research units (1970).

These ideas are similar to those of L-M theory. Nevertheless, they are less precisely arranged in Galtung's scheme than in L-M theory. L-M theory clearly defines the stand-alone element in a system as the most primitive. Galtung's scheme makes a loose connection between the research unit and variables. He connects variables and values in the same fashion as L-M theory. Galtung's research unit (stand-alone element) could be the entire state of an entity. L-M theory always forces the stand-alone element (in terms of which all other things are described) to be the most fundamental element in the system, a L-M theory state. That action avoids the assigning of numbers to vaguely understood systems as surrogates without comparing a system's most fundamental units to an understood measurement scale or assessment standard.

The same investigatory processes apply to management. The final goal of management investigations is the direct and indirect reason for good or poor results. Management investigations may be described with the same kinds of terms, that is, with entities, variables and values of variables, and with the relations among these terms. Managers of organization-level living systems can investigate both internal problems and environmental problems (those concerning interactions with communities, societies, and supranational systems) with similar methods and in common dimensions.

Statistics employs similar concepts. The data treated by statistical methods are divided into statistical entities corresponding to L-M theory entities and Galtung's research units, statistical variables corresponding to selected dimensions, and values of statistical variables that describe the states of the research units. If, therefore, the observations are presented in a form of statistical units, variables, and their values, they can be treated by the apparatus of statistics (Vasama and Vartia 1972). Statistical terms are thus analogical to the tripartite division of terms into variables, values of variables, and entities (Figure 3.1).

Pure mathematics also employs such concepts. In the theory of relation and function, for instance, the data, together with their values, are divided into ordinates and arguments. The values of ordinates and arguments are examined as pairs, and the connection between the members of these pairs as well as the relations of functions are relations in the above sense. When mathematical methods are applied in practice, however, the ordinates and arguments receive certain values for each item of the population under examination. The items possess certain values in ordinates and arguments. The items, and thus the population to which they belong, correspond once more to research units or entities. Again, the mathematical apparatus contains a similar division into terms and relations (Figure 3.4).

The same method of thinking reoccurs in the concepts of computer science. This may be envisioned by thinking of the classical computer report, where each set of data or row contains information about one case, item, unit, and so forth, corresponding to our entity. Each column or combination of columns represents variables. The values in these columns denote the values of variables. When the raw data has been reduced to a form compatible with the three term categories (entities, variables, and values), they may be processed by computers.

The analyst needs ways to organize phenomena so that it can be expressed by means of those three terms and the relations among them. Such organization opens investigations to the full benefits of mathematical and computational methods.

Systems theory also should operate with terms and relations (Figure 3.4). Terms are either entities (matters that are described or investigated), variables (attributes on which these matters are examined), or values (dimensions of these matters). Relations consist of different kinds of connections among these terms, including influence, coexistence, definition, and membership. The latter are the logico-mathematical concepts of systems theory. They reveal how everyday prosaic observations regarding events and episodes, together with their attributes, can be presented in a systemic manner.

SOCIAL SCIENCES	COMPUTERS	STATISTICS MATHEMATICS	LOGICO-MATHEMATICAL BASIC CONCEPTS	
			MAIN CATEG.	SUBCATEG.
Research unit	Event Case	Research object Statistical unit	TERMS	Entity
Variable	Variable Column or column field in the computer report	Property Characteristic Statistical variable Ordinate Argument		Variable
Value of variables Attributes	Value of variable Sign in the computer report	Measure describing a property Values of ordinates or arguments		Value of variable
Relations (depen- dence, influ- ence, covari- ance, etc.)	Relations Dependences Programs	Relation Dependence Function	RELATIONS	Coexis- tence Influence Defini- tion Member- ship

Figure 3.4
Basic Concepts of the Social Sciences, Computers, and Mathematics and Their Counterparts in Systems Theory

QUALITATIVE/QUANTITATIVE/MATHEMATICAL DISTINCTION

It is commonly accepted that a manager must be able to digest qualitative, quantitative, and mathematical information, although the precise meaning of these concepts may not be completely clear. Qualitative and quantitative, for instance, are defined differently in various connections. We use the same distinction between them that is used in chemistry.

Qualitative chemical analysis clarifies what kinds of elements, compounds, or impurities may be found in a material, whereas quantitative analysis gives the amounts involved. Similarly, the peculiar and essential character of the concept at hand is termed *quality*. Thus, qualitative research answers such questions as what kind of entities, values, and variables may be found in the phenomenon under consideration, and which of them exist together.

Quantity refers to characteristics that can be expressed in terms of amount, frequency, and the like—cardinal values. Thus, quantitative research explains how many entities can be found, how often a value occurs, or how often certain concepts go together.

Mathematics is the science of numbers—their operations, interrelations, generalizations, abstractions, and spatial configurations. That definition includes their structure, measurement relationships, and restatements. Mathematical methods operate with numbers. Information must therefore be quantified, and not merely translated into logico-mathematical concepts, before mathematical methods can be applied.

The scope of social science data, therefore, also is divided into qualitative and quantitative areas, that is, into one area where mathematics works and one where it does not. We therefore need a systems theory that is simultaneously qualitative and quantitative, logical and mathematical.

MATHEMATICS

The above reasoning means that mathematics plays a crucial role in the growth of scientific social knowledge in general and in the management of firms in particular. Many pragmatic reasons may be given for that, including the following:

1. Mathematical, statistical, and computational methods use an unambiguous near-universal language of abstract symbols.
2. The conceptual framework of mathematics makes it possible to detect inconsistencies and ambiguities in higher levels of abstractions.
3. Mathematics expresses complex information concisely. Highly complex objects often cannot be described usefully without such information reduction.
4. A high degree of consensus among mathematicians on mathematical language and rules exists.
5. Mathematics is easily combined with computers to save time and effort.

Mathematical methods "produce" more information regarding the relations among terms found in qualitative analysis. Qualitative analysis, for instance, produces information on influential relations only in terms of *ceteris-paribus*, that is, with regard to variable pairs. Statistical methods allow the collection of information about the co-influence of several variables on some other variable. With the help of statistical methods, the analyst can obtain multidimensional or *ceteris-imparibus* information. We have put *produce* in quotation marks, because mathematical methods actually do not produce any new information with respect to the raw data matrix. They merely transform it into a more compact visual or explicit form.

Mathematical methods thus have at least three different functions, which may be defined as: making results more concise, visualizing results, and producing new information concerning multidimensional phenomena and high levels of quantitativity.

RESTRICTIONS OF MATHEMATICAL METHODS

Notwithstanding their usefulness, mathematical methods also have severe disadvantages. Their domain is rather limited compared with that of the qualitative approach, because they impose certain conditions on the material.

Sometimes the number of observations to be examined is so large that the investigator is able to organize only part—a sample—of the total. Inferring characteristics from the sample to the unexamined part requires that the sample fulfill the conditions of statistical representativeness. In many practical studies this is not the case. The use of mathematical methods is not therefore possible and does not satisfy scientific requirements.

This limitation also applies, to some extent, to qualitative methods. One can, however, draw more far-reaching conclusions qualitatively than quantitatively on the basis of an unrepresentative sample. This means that investigators must be satisfied with qualitative results of the type "opinions a, b, and c have been expressed," because they cannot obtain reliable information in the form: "x percent have expressed opinion a, y percent opinion b, and z percent opinion c." The use of mathematical methods sometimes is excluded by the requirements of representativeness.

Many statistical methods require other conditions that limit their applicability. These conditions include:

1. The number of variables may not exceed the number of observations, or there must be a minimum number of observations for each variable.
2. The total number of variables may not be very great. Fifty variables is the absolute maximum for certain multidimensional methods, while for some it is only twenty or even ten.
3. Some methods require that the probability distribution of observations be normal.
4. Some methods can be applied only if all the variables have a ratio scale.
5. Some methods require that the dependencies among variables be linear.

Such restrictions often force research into excessive simplification. Too many factors have to be regarded as constants, and too many must be ignored because of the limited capacity of the mathematical apparatus. If misapplied, mathematical methods can result in simplistic rather than simplified views of the complex phenomena in a manager's environment.

With respect to these simplifying restrictions, mathematical methods may be divided roughly into two categories. Those operating under simple restrictions set hardly any other condition than that the information to be computed is quantitative; these methods range from fundamental arithmetical processes to cross tabulation. Those operating under sophisticated restrictions include such

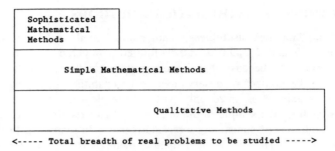

```
<----- Total breadth of real problems to be studied ----->
```

Figure 3.5
Domain of Qualitative and Mathematical Methods

procedures as canonic and factor analysis. The respective ranges of qualitative and mathematical methods therefore may be represented as in Figure 3.5. Qualitative systems, theories, and methods in principle may be applied to the whole range, but sophisticated methods are applicable only to those meeting the specific conditions. Many important practical problems lie beyond the scope of any mathematical method.

We attempt to counter these drawbacks by constructing a systems theory that is simultaneously mathematical and premathematical, quantitative and qualitative. It therefore can be applied to all kinds of phenomena, regardless of their quantitative character, but it also permits and encourages using mathematical methods when appropriate conditions are fulfilled. Even more importantly, it prepares information in a systemic logico-mathematical form, guaranteeing that the applicability of mathematics and computers is as broad as possible.

SUMMARY OF L-M THEORY PREMATHEMATICAL CONTENTS

A pure system identifies certain arrangements in which elements may change without changing the arrangement. The global arrangement that L-M theory identifies is the main principle of qualitative, premathematical thinking and of mathematical thinking. In L-M theory that principle is blended into a comprehensive logico-mathematical structure.

The main characteristics of the premathematical part of L-M theory are:

I. Operation with logico-mathematical concepts in order to conform with mathematical and other quantitative methods.
II. Means to construct concept hierarchies in order to combine the theories with concrete phenomena and to allow shifts in the aggregate level, that is, movement between the micro and macro levels.

III. Means to construct networks in order to combine individual hypotheses and definitions into more holistic compilations as well as into those spanning different scientific disciplines.

IV. Operational instructions on how to apply the theoretical way of thinking in practice.

    A. Analytical methods show how verbal or linguistic concepts are translated into logico-mathematical ones, and vice versa. These, in turn, divide into two parts:

        1. the syntactic part demonstrating how factual statements may be broken down to discover their meaning, and

        2. the *semantic* part showing how concept definitions can be broken down into elements and compared with each other.

    B. Combination methods show how the results of analysis can be combined into hierarchies and networks.

    C. *Synthetical methods* show how new concepts can be produced by the combination of those concepts available in the scientific literature. These methods, in turn, are either

        1. *semantic* (how to compare concept definitions; how to standardize them; how to formulate new definitions, verbal standards, and other semantic operations), or

        2. *syntactic* (how the concepts encountered in research findings and analysis results can be formulated into practical applications and popularized).

MATHEMATICS FROM THE PREMATHEMATICS PERSPECTIVE

The operations described above can be carried out manually. They are either qualitative or so simple that more sophisticated methods are not necessary. But statistical and mathematical methods also would be helpful. Derivatives, a mathematical form of dependencies, can be calculated more easily than the awkward manual premathematical forms. In many other problems, however, mathematics is not just helpful but necessary. The premathematical logic discussed in this book is completely compatible with mathematical logic. Consequently, management observation and communication theory can incorporate sophisticated mathematical methods as needed.

INFORMATION

L-M theory views information broadly. LST defines information more exactly and with emphasis on concrete systems.

L-M theory conceives information as a body of knowledge describing observations, either directly or indirectly, or derived from hearsay. It may thus be gathered by the information holders themselves or through communication with other people. It can be based on investigation or imagination. Its content may be discovered in nature, like most of the knowledge of natural science, or it may be based on conventions among people, as is the case with definitions or agreements.

Management information is given by means of the three categories of values, variables, and entities (Figure 3.1). According to L-M theory there are also three respective languages: value language, variable language, and entity language. In value language the information is given by the values of variables; in variable language by means of variables and the relations among their values; and in entity language by entities and the interrelations of the variables comprising them.

Practically every piece of information can be given in all three of these languages (Figure 3.6). A statement that reads in value language "His pay is high, because his output is high," reads in variable language "Level of pay depends on amount of output," and in entity language "Pay depends on output." These languages seldom are quite separate, but most statements contain elements

VALUE LANGUAGE	ORIGINAL	"His pay is high, because his output is high."
	INTERPRETIVE	"High pay" is because "output is high" the effect <----- is the cause."
	FORMALISTIC	High pay <-----> High output
VARIABLE LANGUAGE	ORIGINAL	"Level of pay depends on level of output."
	INTERPRETIVE	"Level of pay" **depends** and "level of is the dependent <----- output" is the variable independent
	FORMALISTIC	Level of pay <------------> Amount of output
ENTITY LANGUAGE	ORIGINAL	"Pay depends on output!"
	INTERPRETIVE	The entity **influenced** by the entity "pay" is <------- "output"
	FORMALISTIC	Pay <------> Output

Figure 3.6
Propositions Expressed in Value, Variable, and Entity Language

of each language. In the analytical process, however, they are kept separate, since, according to L-M theory, all of them have practical importance.

L-M theory examines any communication as information without limiting the information to that observed in the concrete processes of organizations. LST defines information in concrete processes as the patterns of arrangement in physical space and order over time of their subsystems and components.

Five terms clarify the meaning LST gives the term *information: Structure* is the arrangement of an organization's components at a given moment. *Process* is all action over time and is divided usefully into functions and history. *Function* is readily reversible action that changes structure over time. *History* is less readily reversible action that changes both structure and function over time. The term state means structure and process taken together. In concrete systems, particularly living ones, structure and process actually cannot be separated: one cannot exist without the other. Nobody has experienced the ultimate instant.

The term state consequently is defined differently by L-M theory and LST. State in LST includes changes over time and is called *fluxuous steady state.* The term structure in LST is equivalent to the term state in L-M theory. It is possible, however, to identify a L-M theory state at a moment or for a period. The state of a period necessarily would contain change. Such a state would be consistent with a LST state.

Information about concrete organizations is about their states. Management controls the actions of organizations—their processes. Consequently, management information is process-intensive. The information that L-M theory discovers is information about the concrete processes of organizations and their environments. Management observation and communication theory attempts to sort that information from the many fictions able managers dream for the future. Information about concrete processes then may be used to evaluate which dreams can be realized as the organization moves through time.

SUMMARY

The concepts defined in this chapter are applied in the following chapters. At first reading they may seem difficult to understand. They are not. As stated before, managers typically work at the overall theory a piece at a time. The concepts are precise enough to be applied in detail. How they interrelate also is indicated precisely. That precision makes it possible to build an integrated general theory of management, from the bottom to the top, that can be customized for particular organizations.

REFERENCES

Galtung, J. (1970). *Theory and methods of social research.* Kristianstad.
Klir, G. J. (1985). *Architecture of systems problem solving.* New York: Plenum Press.

Lazarsfield, P. F. (1937). Some remarks on the typological procedures in social research. *Zeitschrift fur sozial forschung* 6: Helsinki, 119–39.

Miller, J. G. (1978). *Living systems*. New York: McGraw-Hill.

Swanson, G. A., and J. G. Miller. (1989). *Measurement and interpretation in accounting: A living systems theory approach.* Westport, Conn.: Greenwood Press.

Troncale, L. R. (1985). Towards a consensus glossary of systems concepts. In *Systems inquiring: Theory, philosophy, methodology,* Proceedings Society for General Systems Research International Conference, Los Angeles, May 27–31, pp. 14–17.

Vasama, P., and Y. Vartia. (1972). *Johdatus tilastotieteeseen.* Helsinki: Gaudeamus.

von Bertalanffy, L. (1950). An outline of general systems theory. *British Journal for the Philosophy of Science* 1: 134–65.

4

How to Construct Backdrops

Management is an information-processing component of organizations. Specifically, it receives information transmissions from various other information-processing components and transmits to them the information that controls the organization.

That information consists of terms and relations that describe the concrete processes of organizations as well as hypothetical systems devised in the brains of people. Sorting the information into that concerning hypothetical systems and that concerning concrete processes is a major problem. Once sorted, evaluating the influence of various hypothetical systems on the concrete processes is sometimes even more problematic.

This chapter discusses ways of organizing the relatively unorganized terms of typical communications in organizations. That task is accomplished by constructing backdrops for individual observations. Techniques are introduced first to identify the terms and the relationships that comprise communications about individual observations, and then to examine them with reference to similar terms in a particular language or other conceptual system. Constructing such backdrops focuses on terms.

Terms are defined as expressions that describe objects having separate and distinct existences. Types of terms are values (describing states), variables (collections of mutually exclusive values), and entities (collections of variables). The discussion begins with the most basic elements of systems, states, and progresses through variables and entities (Figure 3.2).

VARIABLES AND THEIR VALUES

Variables have two important characteristics: mutually exclusive and collectively exhaustive sets of values.

When we observe the world, we notice states of affairs. If we say, "Our good friend Mr. Albertson is always complaining about everything," such states would be "our good friend," "Mr.," "Albertson," and "is always complaining about everything." "Our good friend Mr. Albertson" is the affair these states describe. We make similar observations regarding different affairs. The information obtained is an unorganized body of different values.

To make sense of it the information must be organized. The following method efficiently organizes such information. It first develops mutually exclusive sets of values and then extends the set to be collectively exhaustive.

FROM STATES TO MUTUALLY EXCLUSIVE SETS OF VALUES

A recursive two-step procedure is required to organize descriptions of states of affairs into mutually exclusive sets of values (i.e., variables). The procedure is actually quite simple.

1. Begin by comparing one description to all other descriptions in turn and arranging them in two groups. One group consists of all described states that cannot exist together with the chosen state but may exist instead of it. The other and larger group consists of states that can exist together with the chosen state. Descriptions of states are thus divided into a set of states that are mutually exclusive of each other and a set of states that can exist in tandem with each other. For instance, when the states "always complains about everything," "always seems to be satisfied," "Mr.," and "Mrs." are compared with "always complains about everything," "always seems to be satisfied" is an exclusive state whereas "Mr." and "Mrs." can exist with it.

2. Select another description from the set of states that can exist together as a standard of comparison to again group the other states into a set of states that are mutually exclusive and a set of states that can exist together. Repeat this procedure until all of the original states have been included in at least one of the sets of states that are mutually exclusive of each other. Figure 4.1 illustrates this procedure.

The actual observations being communicated need not include mutually exclusive states. Such states may be sought outside the original set by asking the question, "Is there any state that could exist that excludes this state and is an alternative to it?"

Each set of mutually exclusive states is an attribute of an affair (entity) being examined. Such attributes correspond to sets of values termed *variables*.

Notice that the variables were identified in this procedure from specific states observed in an affair. They were not selected from a general list of variables believed to comprise affairs or entities. It is important to construct variables describing an organization based on the states discovered in its information

```
UNORGANIZED SET OF STATES DESCRIBED - POINT OF DEPARTURE

"is  always  complaining  about  everything"--"Mr."--"good  friend"--"always
satisfied"--"newcomer"--"Mrs."--"bonus  for  seniority  of  0  %"--"old  hand"--
"nonchalant:  indifferent  to  looking  after  his  subordinates"--"lifetimer"--"takes
pains  to  arrange  everything  in  the  best  possible  way  for  his  subordinates"--
"acquaintance"--...  "10% seniority  bonus"--"seniority  bonus  of  20%"
```

Which of these states are mutually exclusive and alternative to the state "always complaining about everything"?	"always seems to be satisfied"!	= basic satisfaction
... "Mr."?	"Mrs."!	= marital status
... "good friend"?	"acquaintance"!	= level of friendship
... "newcomer"?	"old hand" and "lifetimer"	= length of service
... "bonus for seniority of 0 %"?	"10 %" and "20 %"	= bonus for seniority
... "nonchalant: indifferent to looking after his subordinates"?	"takes pains to arrange everything in the best possible way for subordinates"!	= buoyancy regarding needs of subordinates
... "etc."?		

... "OBJECT OF COMPARISON"? SET OF SIMULTANEOUS STATES	SET OF MUTUALLY EXCLUSIVE AND ALTERNATIVE STATES	= SET OF DIMENSIONS OR VARIABLES

Figure 4.1
Organization of an Original Set of Observations into Mutually Exclusive Sets, i.e., Dimensions or Variables

flows. Otherwise, the actual state of an organization may not be describable on a chosen variable.

COLLECTIVELY EXHAUSTIVE SETS

After the variables have been identified from information about the actual states, an exhaustive collection of values that comprise each variable should be

	TOTAL RANGE OF SETS OF MUTUALLY EXCLUSIVE (INTERCHANGEABLE STATES OF AFFAIRS)					WHAT SHOULD THE VARIABLE BE NAMED?
Newcomer	Missing (has served some time)	Missing (average service years)		Old hand	Lifetimer	SENIORITY
Bonus for Seniority	Missing (5 %)	10 %		Missing (15 %)	20 %	BONUS FOR SENIORITY
Performer	Missing (1st line supervisor)	2nd line supervisor	Middle manager	Missing (manager)	Missing (executive manager)	ORGANI- ZATIONAL POSITION
Mr.		Missing (Miss)		Mrs.		MARITAL STATUS OR SEX
Missing	Slightly unsatisfactory		Missing	Good	Outstanding	PERFORMANCE LEVEL
Nonchalant. Indifferent to looking after his subordinates	Missing (to some extent looks after)			Takes pains to arrange everything in the best possible way		BUOYANCY TOWARD SUBORDINATES
Always complaining about everything	Missing (Normal)			Always satisfied		BASIC SATISFACTION

Figure 4.2
Values of Variables Covering the Scope of Possible States from the Minimal to the Maximal States

identified (Figure 4.2). The characteristics of the values comprising a variable may be examined by asking the following questions in order:

1. How can the comparative and superlative degrees be used with this set, either in a natural way or in a conceivable way? This question determines the scale that may be used for measuring the states involved. If the values of the variable are only different, a nominal scale is the highest level of measurement achievable. Knowing that one state is greater than another, but not knowing by how much, advances the measurement level to an ordinal scale. Knowing how much it is greater advances the measurement level to interval. Variables may be measured on ratio scales if how much greater one state is compared to another is known, and an absolute absence of the variable can occur.

With reference to the "seniority" set, for example, the answer to this question is that the superlative degree can be used. Among a group of colleagues, some have served longer than others. Someone has served the longest time, and someone has served the shortest time.

2. Which observed state is the greatest degree of *x*, when *x* denotes the

variable (attribute). In the case of seniority, the state *lifetimer* corresponds to the greatest degree state.

3. Is there any conceivable state that represents the variable to an even greater degree? What is the maximum possible state, either inside or outside the original set? In this case, the answer is lifetimer, which is the longest service imaginable.

The maximum end of the set range may be determined in that way. Analogous questions may be asked about the other extreme:

4. Which state represents the least degree?

5. What is the absolute minimum state that either is mentioned in the observed set or is conceivable?

The parameters of a variable are discovered in that way. The next questions concern coverage.

6. Do the states included at this point cover the total range between the maximum and minimum states?

7. If not, which states are missing? In the example, such missing states might be "has served some time" and "average service."

8. What should the name of this set (variable) be? After a set has been identified, a name that is easily associated with the set should be selected.

VARIABLES

By this method, the original set of mutually exclusive and alternative states has been described by values in a collectively exhaustive set covering the total possible variation of a variable. The term *variable,* thus, has been methodically defined as a set of mutually exclusive and alternative, collectively exhaustive values. The values represent the states a particular variable can describe. Each value is a step on a scale or standard.

Such variables describe different aspects of the entity. They may

- denote a quality of the entity such as production manager or clerk in the variable job;
- indicate its quantity by means of exact measurements, such as "Has served our company three years," or through judgments, such as "newcomer";
- specify one thing as distinct from another, such as female and male, or Albertson and Bernardson; and
- describe events such as "Reads newspapers during peak office hours" or "Is always complaining about everything."

Almost all kinds of linguistic concepts can describe states thus. For instance, states may be described by

- adjectives, such as blue or yellow, when they are used as different values of the variable "color";

- nouns such as Mrs. and Mr., when they are conceived of as values of sex or marital status;

- proper nouns such as Albertson and Bernardson, when the relevant variable is "last name";

- verbs such as opposes and supports, when they are used as expressions of the variable "position with regard to an issue";

- clauses such as "It is wrong that . . ." and "It is right that . . ." when they represent the variable "attitudes toward an object"; and

- sentences such as, "The smallest change or even suspected change leads to sit-down strikes in his unit. It's like a volcano. You never know when it will erupt," or "I can't remember any complaints by the union officials or shop stewards about his unit. He can discuss and solve problems before they become a question of prestige," when the sentences are interpreted as different levels of the variable "working harmony."

REASONS FOR OBSERVING

Organizations are multidimensional. Managers typically do not have only one reason for observing organizational processes. People observe the world with respect to dimensions (variables) from the following five different viewpoints (Figures 4.3):

1. *Neutral observation.* The state of an entity is determined solely with reference to relevant variables. These observations may be estimates (assessments), such as, "*A* has served this company rather a long time," or more exact measurements, such as, "As of today, *A* has served our company for 24 years, 10 months, and 5 days."

2. *Comparison with objectives and needs.* Neutral observations also are compared with objectives, aesthetic ideas, needs, or other images people have in their minds regarding a desired state. This kind of comparison includes such expressions as, "Our production has met the objectives set for costs, profits, and marketing," "This product is really beautiful," and "This kind of activity is really unnecessary."

3. *Comparison with an ideal.* The state may be compared with a theoretical, absolute, or otherwise faultless state. Statements such as, "Performance is near maximum human capacity," "In this chemical mill the yield is 98 percent, 2 percent less than the theoretical maximum," and "The amount of avoidable costs is 5 percent," are comparisons with an ideal.

4. *Appraisal.* The state is evaluated with reference to its usefulness, scarcity, and difficulty of achievement, the sacrifices it has required, or different combina-

1ST PHASE			2ND PHASE			3RD PHASE			4TH PHASE			5TH PHASE		
1ST QUESTION	1ST COMPAR.	1ST CONCL.	2ND QUESTION	2ND COMPAR.	2ND CONCL.	3RD QUESTION	3RD COMPAR.	3RD CONCL.	4TH QUESTION	4TH COMPAR.	4TH CONCL.	5TH QUESTION	5TH COMPAR.	5TH CONCL.
HOW DOES IT RELATE TO AVERAGE?	Exceeds!	ABOVE AVERAGE		Exceeds!	BETTER THAN SATISFACTORY		None!	FAULTLESS OUTSTANDING		Extremely difficult and demanding!	VERY VALUABLE AND WORTHY		It is worth reinforcement!	REWARD, RECOGNITION, PAY RAISE, PROMOTION, RETURN SERVICE
	Meets!	AVERAGE	DOES IT MEET MY OBJECTIVES?	Meets!	SATISFACTORY	HOW MUCH ROOM IS THERE FOR IMPROVEMENT?	Some!	GOOD	HOW DIFFICULT IS IT TO ACHIEVE? WHAT IS IT WORTH?	Normally demanding and difficult!	NORMAL	WHAT KIND OF RESPONSE DOES IT DESERVE?	No comments!	NOTHING
	Fails to meet!	BELOW AVERAGE		Fails to meet!	UNSATISFACTORY		Very much!	INADEQUATE		Extremely easy!	WORTHLESS		It is worth avoiding!	PUNISHMENT DISAPPROVAL PAY CUT, DEMOTION, REVENGE

Figure 4.3
How People Observe, Compare Observations with Objectives, Evaluate Their Worth, and Decide What Responses Are Deserved

57

tions of these. Expressions such as "This job is really demanding," "This subject is taboo and, therefore, cannot be discussed," and "These tasks are crucial for the welfare of the whole company" evaluate the worth of the state in this sense.

5. *Choice of response.* What kind of response the observed state deserves is decided. The statement "Something is admirable" means "It earns our admiration." Calling it criminal means "It deserves a punishment prescribed by law." The statement "Cost leakage is so high that it should be looked into" suggests that it merits investigation, and the declaration "He is entitled to a pay raise" suggests the response "pay raise."

All five viewpoints are not relevant to every kind of dimension (variable), although they are to most of them. They almost always apply in organizations where the interaction between individuals and collectives plays a leading role. When individuals observe the behavior of their colleagues, they almost always compare them with their own standards, and they evaluate their colleagues' behavior with their own images of ideal behavior and respond.

They thus go through the whole repertoire. In organizations, performances continually are appraised, results evaluated, and people rewarded with pay raises and promotions or punished by reprimands, pay cuts, demotions, and discharge.

Including the entire repertoire considers all observations from the perspective of human interactions. The responses are acts of distribution: when people are rewarded their well-being is improved, and when they are punished their well-being suffers. From our point of view, this means that a general systems theory should provide managers with methods that identify all five of those kinds of observations, evaluations, and choices.

ESTIMATES AND MEASUREMENTS

Within any dimension (variable), observations or comparisons may be made at different degrees of exactness. Estimates (assessments) and measurements may be distinguished on that quality (Figure 4.4).

In observations, the least exact level is a subjective and rough estimate, followed by assessments and measurements on increasingly precise scales. Observations such as "A produces extremely cheaply" or "B's costs are higher, but still moderate" are estimates by observers comparing actual costs with ideas of average ones in their own heads. Alternatively, observations may be given in exact figures that were obtained by measurements and exact calculations.

The expression "Costs are above objectives" is an estimate. When the deviation from objectives is given in exact figures, the statement incorporates a measurement.

Expressions of appraisal, such as "requires really vigorous effort," represent

PHASE	ESTIMATE	MEASUREMENT
NEUTRAL OBSERVATION	A produces extremely cheaply	$4.9/unit
	B's costs are higher, but still moderate	$8.2/unit
COMPARISON WITH OBJECTIVES	A's costs are below what we estimated and	$1.1/unit lower than our objective
	B's costs are higher	$2.2/unit higher
COMPARISON WITH AN IDEAL	Even if A's costs are low, there is room for improve-ment	According to our calculations the absolute minimum is $4.0. Thus A still has a cost leakage of $0.9/unit
	and for B still more	B's cost leakage is at the moment $4.2/unit
APPRAISAL	It requires really vigorous effort before one can reach A's level of costs	A's cost level corresponds to perfor-mance level 9 on the performance level scale
	B's cost level can be reached rather easily	B's level is 5
RESPONSE	A is entitled to a considerable bonus	A's bonus is $5,000 this year
	B deserves hardly any bonus	B's bonus is $1,000

Figure 4.4
Formulation of Observations as Estimates and as Measurements

estimates, while the number of clock hours an employee works, and the numbers used to keep time and delimit the distance in an athletic decathlon are examples of measuring the significance or scarcity of some act.

Examples of responses can be found most easily within wage administration. All verbal opinions and demands regarding pay systems are generally some kind of estimate, whereas the official pay systems, such as a seniority rule, included in many agreements, exemplify measurement rules.

TWO KINDS OF HIERARCHIES

An essential idea of L-M theory is that information about states is organized by means of two kinds of hierarchies: *part hierarchies* and *membership hierarchies*. The two kinds are distinguished from each other based on the quality of *mutual exclusivity*.

Hierarchies in which larger units are exact "sums" of their subunits are called part hierarchies. Every subunit has an exactly defined location within a larger unit in such hierarchies. The smaller units are organic parts of the larger units. Part hierarchies are values arranged into mutually exclusive and alternative, collectively exhaustive sets. They are used to divide perceived states into smaller measurable units or combine them into larger ones. They are concerned with the different possible scales or standards on which a particular variable may be measured or assessed.

Membership hierarchies are concerned with organizing particular variables into larger and larger sets. Each variable is a loose member of a larger unit and not an organic part of it.

Figure 4.5 compares the two types of hierarchies. They have two features in common. One feature is that each concept at a higher level (i.e., the superconcept) is divided into two or more subconcepts. The second is that division is based on some distinguishing feature among subconcepts or, conversely, the association of some similar feature shared by all the subconcepts being combined. Critical differences also exist. The subconcepts are mutually exclusive in part hierarchies and are simultaneous in membership hierarchies. The functions of the two types also differ. Part hierarchies serve changes in precision, and membership hierarchies serve changes in levels of abstraction. Part hierarchies indicate values of variables describing states, and membership hierarchies identify qualities of variables.

The functional differences are paramount. Part hierarchies refine the precision of observing the concrete process of organizations, and membership hierarchies connect information about those processes to management theory. Both functions are necessary for managing organizations.

PRECISION

States may be measured with differing degrees of precision on many dimensions. This means that the size of the measuring unit varies. The smaller it is, the more precise are the observations, and the smaller the nuances that can be distinguished from each other. For instance, time can be measured in years, months, weeks, days, hours, minutes, seconds, or in even smaller units.

Exactness and precision are two different things. Exactness distinguishes between measurements and assessments (estimates). Precision distinguishes among different measurement scales that may be used to identify the values of a

	PART HIERARCHIES (e.g. state hierarchy)	MEMBERSHIP HIERARCHIES (e.g. variable hierarchy)
SIMILARITIES	1) Each concept of the upper hierarchic level (i.e. superconcept) is divided into two or more subconcepts.	
	2) The division is based on some distinguishing feature between the subconcepts and the association of some similar feature shared by all of the subconcepts to be combined.	
DISTINCTIONS		
Exclusiveness	Subconcepts are mutually exclusive	...are not mutually exclusive but simultaneous
Exhaustiveness	Subconcepts are collectively exhaustive	...are not so, except in extreme cases
Similarity	Subconcepts are similar to each other	...are not similar, except for the shared feature
Exactness of location	Each subconcept has an exact place given by means of an ordinal number etc.	The location of each subconcept is vague, and its position in the conceptual space is based on convention
Type of relation between super- and subconcept	Part relation: subconcepts are organic parts of the superconcepts with an exact spatiotemporal location	Membership relation: subconcepts are loose members of the set with rather arbitrary location
FUNCTION	Change of precision	Connection between theory and practice (real life)
when moving		Reduction of body of variables
upward	Decrease in precision toward macro	Abstraction Widening of scope
downward	Increase in precision toward micro	Concretization Application Operationalization Increase in detail

Figure 4.5
Similarities and Distinctions Between the Part and Membership Hierarchies

variable. All measurement scales are exact within measurement error limits. Although it is technically possible to measure elements in higher-order human systems (such as organizations) in terms of very precise scales, scales that measure those systems themselves are less precise than scales that measure the lower-order systems that are their elements. Organizations, for example, may be measured on the attribute biological cell activity in terms of accepted scale units. However, such measurements do not describe an organization in any important way, because while the cell processes of a janitor and of a corporate president are similar, the functions of those organisms in organizations are very different.

From our point of view, the different measuring units of a variable form a part hierarchy in which the units become smaller from level to level (Figure 4.6). At each level, the units are the same. So, for instance, a year is the period required for one revolution of the earth around the sun, a month is the period required for one revolution of the moon around the earth, and a day is the period for one

MEASURING UNIT/"ORIGO"	HIERARCHY
YEAR (period required for one revolution of the earth around the sun) ORIGIN Anno Domini	1985 T_{1985}
MONTH (period required for one revolution of the moon around the earth) ORIGIN Turn of the year	JANUARY .... DECEMBER $T_{1985.1}$ $T_{1985.12}$
WEEK (cycle of seven days) ORIGIN Turn of the year	1. .... 52. $T_{1985.1.1}$ $T_{1985.1.52}$
DAY (period required for one rotation of the earth around its axis) ORIGIN Turn of the week	SUNDAY .... SATURDAY $T_{1985.1.1.1}$ $T_{1985.1.1.7}$
HOUR (the 24th part of a day) ORIGIN Turn of the day	1. .... 24. $T_{1985.1.1.1.1}$ $T_{1985.1.1.1.24}$
MINUTE (the 60th part of an hour)	1. .... 60. $T_{1985.1.1.1.1.1}$ $T_{1985.1.1.1.1.60}$
....	... .

<---- PRECISION
LIGHTNESS OF EXPRESSION ---->

NOTE: Each place on the continuum is expressed by means of the level of measuring units and their identities, i.e., their "last names" and "first names."

Figure 4.6
Measuring Units in the Form of a Hierarchy

rotation of the earth on its axis. At each level, each unit has a relation to other units at the same level. This is determined by their location with regard to other units at the same level. So, for instance, January is the first month and February is the second one, and 1985 is the fifth year of the decade 1980.

This means that all the definitions of measuring units and their means of identification form a multidimensional set of coordinates that give the results of every measurement. To specify the exact moment of time in minutes, the time "space" may be described as six dimensional (Figure 4.7): year, month, week, day, hour, and minute.

MEASURING UNIT	YEAR	MONTH	WEEK	DAY	HOUR	MINUTE
	Period required for one revolution of earth around sun	Period required for one revolution of moon around earth	Cycle of seven days	Period required for one rotation of earth around its axis	The 24th part of a day	The 60th part of an hour
MEANS OF IDENTIFI-CATION ORDINAL NUMBER	Ordinal number anno domini	Ordinal number from the New Year	Ordinal number from the New Year	Ordinal number from the turn of the week	Ordinal number from midnight	Ordinal number from the turn of the hour
1 2 3 . 7 . 12 . 24 . 52 . 60 . 1985 . 1992	1 2 3 . 7 . 12 . 24 . 52 . 60 . 1985 . 1992	January February March . July . December	1 2 3 . 7 . 12 . 24 . 52	Sunday Monday Tuesday . Saturday .	1 2 3 . 7 . 12 . 24	1 2 3 . 7 . 12 . 24 . 52 . 60
For instance: NOW	1992	July	31	Wednesday	18	20

NOTE: Location is expressed by means of its ordinal number. Because weeks do not begin precisely on the New Year, the numbers in the week column are approximations.

Figure 4.7
Description of a State of Time

The result of measurement is indicated by means of an ordinal number giving a position within the basic measuring units (e.g., years), and then within its subunits (months, weeks, days, hours, and minutes). This subdivision and identification may be described, for example, by a subscript code. The position of the unit in the subscript number refers to its hierarchic level. Thus, for instance, 1985.1 and 1985.2 are months, 1985.1.1 and 1985.12.52 are weeks, and 1985.2.5.2 and 1985.12.50.3 are weekdays. Thus, the position indicates the "last name" of the unit: year, month, week, day, and so forth; and the numbers (the "first name") indicate the unit's identity (e.g., 1985.3 means March 1985, and 1985.12.50.3 means Tuesday in the fiftieth week which occurs in December 1985.

HIERARCHY OF VARIABLES

When the values have been organized into variables, the number of variables often is still too large to be practical. Their number, therefore, should be reduced. This process may be completed by hierarchically arranging them into classes of features that the variables have in common. The resulting hierarchy is a membership hierarchy.

In Figure 4.8, this procedure is exemplified by means of a set of performance criteria used in personnel administration. The example begins with values that are individual judgments regarding the performance level of supervisors. The judgments "I can rely on him" and "I must remember each assignment I give him" are combined into a variable termed *reliability,* defined as the need to be looked after. The judgments "He is able to carry out _____ without asking unnecessary questions" and "He is always asking for advice" are included in the variable termed *independence,* meaning the need to be advised. These are variables of the first order. Many other variables may occur at this level, such as faultlessness and neatness.

Reliability and independence have in common the property of describing how easily the ratee (the person being rated) is supervised and are, therefore, combined into a variable of the second order termed *flexibility.* The judgments faultlessness and neatness are interpreted as evaluating the mastery of the ratee's job and are consequently combined into a variable termed *skill.* Many other variables may exist at this level, such as the economic efficiency and the organizational climate of the unit led by the ratee.

Since flexibility and skill refer to tasks carried out personally by the ratee, they are combined into the class termed *personal efficiency,* and the two former variables are classified as *efficiency of the ratee's unit.* These variables of the third order are regarded as describing the ratee's total performance level, a variable of the fourth order.

In this way, hundreds of first-order variables are combined into some fifteen

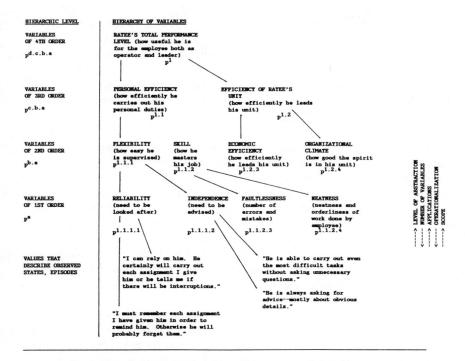

Figure 4.8
Hierarchy of Variables

to twenty variables of the second order. These, in turn, form some two to five third-order variables that combine into one single variable of the fourth order. The number of variables may thus be reduced by means of a membership hierarchy.

The location of each concept in a membership hierarchy may be indicated symbolically, as the measurement unit was given by subscript in the part hierarchy in Figure 4.6. For such membership hierarchies as this, superscripts are used instead of subscripts. For instance, p^a refers to the variables of the first level, $p^{b.a}$ refers to the second level, $p^{c.b.a}$ refers to the third level, and $p^{d.c.b.a}$ refers to the fourth level. Thus, the position in the chain indicates the hierarchical level, which at the same time is the level of abstraction. The terms $p^{1.v.v}$ and $p^{2.v.v}$, for example, indicate the first and second variables at the third level. The longer the string, the more abstract is the variable.

An index thus constructed can be read easily beginning at the top of the hierarchy. In Figure 4.8, for instance, p^1 refers to the first variable at the highest level, $p^{1.1}$ and $p^{1.2}$ are the first and second variables at the next lower level, $p^{1.2.3}$ and $p^{1.2.4}$ are the third and fourth variables at the next lower level, and so forth. In this way, the index chain shows the hierarchical location of each variable in relation to each hierarchical level. Thus, for instance, $p^{1.1.2.4}$ indicates that the fourth variable (neatness) belongs at the next level to variable two (skill). It belongs at the following level to variable one (personal efficiency) and in turn belongs to variable one (ratee's total performance level) at the highest level.

This method of indexing allows each variable to be defined. If the shared features (i.e., the definitions used for combining variables into superconcepts) are written down in the hierarchy (as in Figure 4.8), the superscript number chain helps identify the elements of a definition. Thus, the term reliability ($p^{1.1.1}$) is a variable describing how useful the ratee is for supervisors (p^1) from the viewpoint of how efficiently he carries out his personal duties ($p^{1.1}$). That, in turn, is from the viewpoint of "how easy he is to supervise" ($p^{1.1.1}$).

This membership hierarchy is similar to the part hierarchy of values introduced in Figure 4.6 in connection with precision, although there are some essential differences. In the membership hierarchy, the parallel subconcepts of a common superconcept are not mutually exclusive but in most cases exist simultaneously, whereas in the part hierarchy of values, the subconcepts really are mutually exclusive. Furthermore, the parallel members of this hierarchy are not similar to each other, except for the shared features mentioned in the hierarchy, whereas in the hierarchy of values they are assumed to be similar.

Membership hierarchies identify the quality of a variable, and part hierarchies identify its value. We have suggested that these characteristics of a variable be indicated by means of superscripts and subscripts. The superscripts refer to the quality and the subscripts denote the value of a variable, for example,

$$P^{1.2.1}_{12.1} \qquad P^{\text{seniority}}_{12 \text{ yrs, 2 mo}} \qquad P^{\text{sex}}_{\text{female}} \qquad P^{\text{performance level}}_{\text{high}}$$

We will use these types of hierarchies throughout the rest of this book.

ORGANIZING ENTITIES INTO LARGER SYSTEMS

Until this point Chapter 4 has examined states by organizing the values describing them into variables and by reducing variables into superconcepts. The affairs described by such variables are matters, things, events, and other concrete phenomena or else they are concerns, ideas, or similar concepts. They are characterized by an independent and separate existence in objective or conceptual reality. Such affairs may be entities. Values, variables, and entities are the basic terms used to describe the concrete states of living systems as well as any stand-alone concepts.

According to LST, living systems may be arranged on a hierarchy of increasing complexity where higher levels are physically composed of lower ones. Such a hierarchy is a part hierarchy. That increasing complexity may be described in a manner similar to constructing variables from values. The components that concern managers, however, are usually entities—combinations of variables. Different management decisions might concern different variables of a particular entity. In fact, comparing different entities requires that they be measured or assessed on the same variable, so managers identify variables common to the entities they intend to compare. Because the entities are complex, comparisons on one variable seldom satisfy managers. Consequently, they attempt to combine the results of evaluations on several variables. Those actions require part hierarchies to determine the values of the variables comprising an entity, and membership hierarchies to determine the qualities of these variables.

Because managers usually perceive organizational entities as components, we call part hierarchies that combine entities instead of values into larger systems *aggregate hierarchies*. We retain the term *membership hierarchies* for those that combine variables into superconcepts, because that action is the same whether it is taken in the context of the variables themselves or the entities they comprise.

These hierarchies have the same functions with reference to entities as the part and membership hierarchies have with reference to variables. Symbolic notation similar to that introduced for variables, consequently, can be used for entities. The membership hierarchy, indicating the taxonomic location of an entity idea in the conceptual frame of reference, is described by superscript notation. The aggregate hierarchy, defining the exact location in physical space-time, is described by subscript notation. For example,

$$E_{\text{part hierarchy}}^{\text{membership hierarchy}} \text{ equals } E_{\text{identity}}^{\text{taxonomic location}}, E_{2513\text{-}67}^{\text{person}}, E_{\text{sales}}^{\text{department}}, \text{ or } E_{135}^{\text{room}}.$$

In other words, the upper index defines the quality of an entity, and the lower index reveals its identity.

FROM INDIVIDUAL ENTITIES TO MUTUALLY EXCLUSIVE SETS OF ENTITIES

The basic procedure may be demonstrated with a company's personnel. Beginning with an individual employee, the question, Who is his direct superior? is asked (Figure 4.9). The answer may be, BA is his foreman. We have thus discovered that there is a relationship of subordination between BA and A, and that there is an organizational unit led by a foreman, BA. A is a member of a set, perhaps called a section, led by BA. Since it is fairly common for each person to have only one official superior, the relationship is exclusive, and there is only one section to which A can belong. Next, we complete this mutually exclusive set by

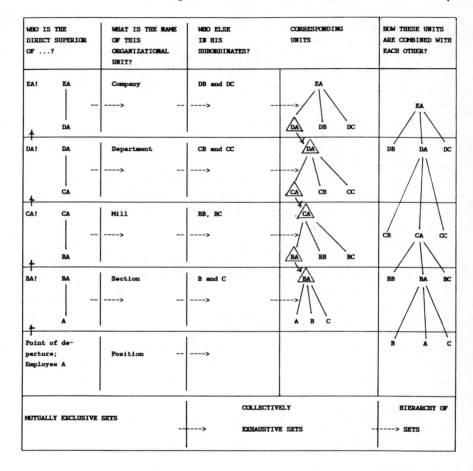

WHO IS THE DIRECT SUPERIOR OF ...?	WHAT IS THE NAME OF THIS ORGANIZATIONAL UNIT?	WHO ELSE IN HIS SUBORDINATES?	CORRESPONDING UNITS	HOW THESE UNITS ARE COMBINED WITH EACH OTHER?
EA! EA ↓ DA	Company	DB and DC	EA / DA DB DC	EA
DA! DA ↓ CA	Department	CB and CC	DA / CA CB CC	DB DA DC
CA! CA ↓ BA	Mill	BB, BC	CA / BA BB BC	CB CA CC
BA! BA ↓ A	Section	B and C	BA / A B C	BB BA BC
Point of departure; Employee A	Position			B A C
MUTUALLY EXCLUSIVE SETS		COLLECTIVELY EXHAUSTIVE SETS		HIERARCHY OF SETS

NOTE: Individual persons are organized into mutually exclusive sets, i.e. organizational units; these units are finalized into exhaustive sets and, lastly, combined into a hierarchy, i.e. an organizational chart.

Figure 4.9
Organizing Entities

asking, Who else beside A is a subordinate of foreman BA. The answer is B and C. A, B, and C together form the whole section led by BA. Those values (that now describe the state of an entity) are a collectively exhaustive set.

The organization of the sections is discovered in a similar manner by asking, Who is the direct superior of BA. The answer may be, CA the mill manager. BB and BC may be other foremen at this mill. Similarly, it may be ascertained that department manager DA is the superior of CA, CB, and CC, who are in charge of their respective mills or divisions, and that DA together with DB and DC are subordinate to executive manager EA.

In the organization of groups led by the first-line supervisors, there may be other groups headed by second-line supervisors. Such groups are formed at different levels of the hierarchy. Many persons belong simultaneously to two different groups. They are subordinate in one group while they are in a leading position in another. These groups may therefore be combined into a hierarchy, as shown in Figure 4.10.

That example demonstrates again that organization proceeds by the same three steps as was the case for states: the descriptions of entities are combined into mutually exclusive sets; these sets are formed into exhaustive sets; then, these sets are combined into a hierarchy.

ENTITY HIERARCHY AS AN AGGREGATE HIERARCHY

The concrete world consists of a hierarchy of systems as described by Miller (1978). Each higher-level system is constituted by lower-level systems. Atoms are composed of particles, molecules of atoms, organelles of molecules, cells of organelles and molecules, organs of cells, organisms or individuals of organs, groups are composed of individuals, and so on. This means, for instance, that the individuals observed (Figure 4.10) are found to be working in sections, that is, ensembles led by a foreman. These groups are organized into departments (divisions of a firm with particular business functions). The departments together form a firm, which might be defined as an association of persons carrying on a commercial or industrial enterprise. For statistical purposes, firms are grouped into distinct sectors by type of business activity. The sectors as a whole form an economy. The sum of all economies forms the world economy. In this way, human beings can be organized into larger and larger units or, as we call them, entities.

There are several entities at each level. Each entity has a separate existence, occupying space in the spatiotemporal universe. This means, in turn, that each of them has an identity. Where human beings are concerned, identity is given by means of a name and other personal data. But at the same time, each person occupies a particular job and may be described by means of that job. Each person has a certain position in this organization. Person A, for instance, is identified either by means of a name or by reference to a job, such as, "This person is the microscopist in the research section led by Dr. A." This means that individual entities at each level have a certain location expressed by means of position.

This also means that, when we speak of working life, the description makes reference to at least two hierarchies, one for persons and the other for activities. A hierarchy of persons is termed an *agent hierarchy,* and an activity hierarchy is

GLOBAL	NATIONAL	SECTOR	COMPANY 1	DEPARTMENT	SECTION	JOBS
			Company 1			Person A
					Research Section	B
		Metal Industry	Company 2	Marketing Department 1		C
						D
			Company 3		Sales Section	E
						F
			Company 4			G
						H
	Nation A	Computer Industry	Company 5		Design Section	I
						K
			Company 6			L
All Mankind				Planning Department 2		M
			Hospital 7			N
					Drawing Section	O
		Health Care	Hospital 8			P
						Q
			Hospital 9			R
					Maintenance Section	S
			Company 10			T
				Production Department 3		U
			Company 11			V
	Nation B	Metal Industry			Operation Section	W
			Company 12			X
						Y
			Company 13			Z

Figure 4.10
Entity Hierarchy as an Aggregate Hierarchy

70

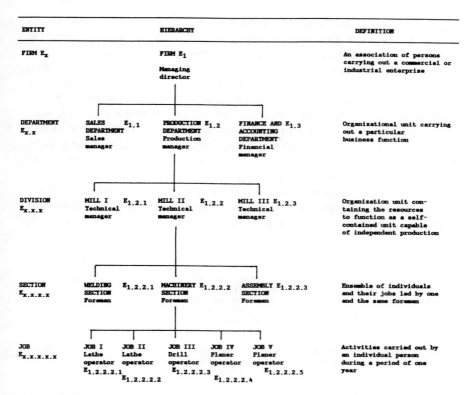

Figure 4.11
**Activity of a Company as a Process Hierarchy, in which the Individual Jobs Are
the Elements**

termed *process hierarchy*. An organizational chart sometimes belongs to the
agent type (as in Figure 4.10) and sometimes belongs to the process type (as in
Figure 4.11). In the latter case, the individual jobs are combined into sections led
by a foreman, the sections into divisions led by middle managers, the divisions
into departments led by managers, and the departments into companies led by an
executive manager.

ENTITIES AND MEMBERSHIP HIERARCHIES

After the entities have been organized into aggregate hierarchies, whether
agency or process, a need for further organization may still exist. Sometimes the
number of individual entities at any aggregate level is too large to examine; their
number then should be reduced. Sometimes there is a theoretical need to classify

them according to their presumed properties. The procedure for doing this is similar to that used for the reduction of variables and forms a membership hierarchy of entities. Thus, for example, individual persons may be divided into welders, turners, foremen, and other groups, according to their occupation (Figure 4.12). These groups may be combined into larger sets, according to the sector of industry in which they work. They may also be divided into wage earners, as opposed to salaried employees. Wage earners and salaried employees, as distinct from entrepreneurs, are both employees inasmuch as they work in the service of an employer. Entrepreneurs and employees form the active part of the population. The passive and active populations together form a nation, the citizens of which may be distinguished from foreigners.

The concept is again the same as that introduced with regard to variables. Entities are arranged into classes by means of shared features. Similar hierarchies may be constructed at each aggregate level. These hierarchies are membership

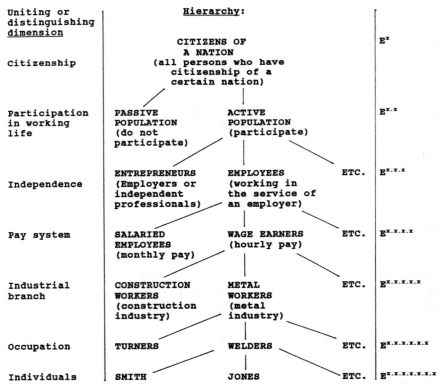

Figure 4.12
Individual Persons as a Membership Hierarchy

hierarchies. The supraentities are loose sets, not organic sums of their members. These hierarchies, too, may be indicated by means of decimal notation in superscripts.

SUMMARY

Chapter 4 provides detailed examples of how the basic stand-alone terms used to communicate in organizations may be analyzed and synthesized to construct backdrops. The backdrops are used for interpreting individual observations of concrete processes and determining what ideas are important to communicators. Chapter 5 extends the L-M theory procedures to those designed to investigate important relationships among multiple observations.

REFERENCE

Miller, J. G. (1978). *Living systems*. New York: McGraw-Hill.

5

How to Use Backdrops in Management

The preceding chapter discussed the basic concepts, terms, and relations, focusing on values, variables, and entities. Those terms are separately identifiable elements. Relations are connections among terms. A relation cannot stand alone. It exists because two or more stand-alone elements are located in some identifiable proximity to one another.

Organizations are composed of separately identifiable elements. However, an organization would not exist if those elements were not interacting and located in a certain fluctuating pattern. An organization, consequently, is more directly described by a set of relations than by a set of the terms. Of course, the relations cannot exist without the terms.

This chapter discusses relations in some depth. Managers are concerned with relations in organizations. Such relations are highly complex. It is actually impossible to stand aloof from an organization and view its relations from a macroperspective. Managers must discover organizational relations from their own spatiotemporal locations within organizations. That action involves viewing the organizational system through a particular part.

We term such partial systems *source systems,* similar to the meaning given by Klir (1985: 35). Source systems differ from entities in that their boundaries are not set by systematically identifying their elements (from value to variable to entity). Instead, managers arbitrarily set the boundaries of source systems, and thus source system boundaries are not necessarily natural or logical. Source systems, consequently, may cut across numerous physical and conceptual boundaries.

That characteristic, if left unchecked, makes it easy to imagine organizational conditions that do not actually exist. To counter that tendency, we force a connection between source systems and individual observations as we did with entity construction. The basic ideas for constructing entities are used to construct source systems, that is, backdrops are constructed from actual observations. Backdrops for source systems, however, are designed to accommodate multiple observations, the typical construct of such systems. Forcing a connection between manager source systems and individual observations may change the source system from the actual one conceived by a manager. That action changes the source system from a private set of relationships believed to exist to a public set that may be validated by other members of the organization through empirical means.

The methods for investigating organizations through source systems are similar to the basic patterns established for investigating variables and entities. The focus of investigation, however, is relationship among multiple observations. That focus requires additional procedures. This chapter progresses from defining source systems through identifying various procedures for investigating relations in organizations.

ORGANIZATIONS AND SOURCE SYSTEMS

As viewed by LST, an organization consists of all concrete component entities, with the important physical relationships among them maintained in relatively narrow ranges (steady state) over an indefinite period. Those processes are influenced by conceptual and abstracted systems in the minds of human components and in the communication media of the organization. Consequently, investigations can be based on viewing organizations as all possible concrete component entities, and all their possible states, at all possible points in time. This configuration makes it possible to identify changes over time (processes), the ultimately critical elements of such higher-order human systems.

Obviously, the entire universe of an organization described by LST is impossible to observe in a single observation. The impossibility arises because an observer cannot be in the past or future at a present moment. Even taking into consideration the influence of conceptual and abstracted systems by viewing organizations as complexities of possible states, including an entire organization in a single study is practically impossible. Such constraints require managers to investigate organizations through more limited sets of observations. Those sets are source systems.

A source system consists of a subject population, a subject topic, and a time period (Figure 5.1). The term *subject population* refers to the limited number of entities subjected to a particular set of observations. Limiting the number of entities included in the observations reduces the set's complexity considerably, but not enough. The entities may contain too many possible variables, so the possible variables may be reduced. The number of dimensions (values) on which variables may be evaluated also may be reduced. The term *subject topic* identi-

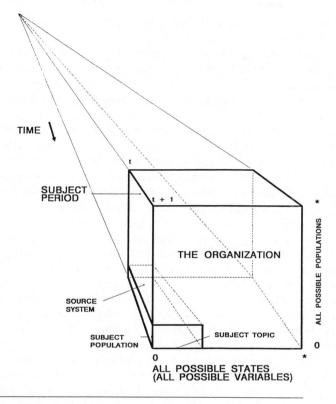

TIME

SUBJECT
PERIOD

THE ORGANIZATION

ALL POSSIBLE POPULATIONS

t

t + 1

SOURCE
SYSTEM

SUBJECT
POPULATION

SUBJECT TOPIC

0

0

ALL POSSIBLE STATES
(ALL POSSIBLE VARIABLES)

NOTE: The source system of a study consists of a subject topic
        regarding the subject population for the subject period of time.

Figure 5.1
A Source System

fies a category to which all possible states, and thus values, are ultimately
reduced for a particular set of observations. The set is further narrowed by
limiting the observation of the subject topic to a specified time period. The result
of all this is to reduce the scope of a set of management observations to a
comprehensible size.

SPATIOTEMPORAL SPACE AND BACKDROP

A source system is a limited set of observations. Source systems are connected
to actual physical states of organizations in a way similar to connecting variables
and entities to such states. Backdrops are constructed with reference to particular

observed states. Nevertheless, source system backdrops anticipate changes in states.

In concrete systems, all change occurs over time, and such change is called process. That condition requires organizational source systems to incorporate the time dimension. Source systems, consequently, are spatiotemporal constructs.

LST calls the location of physical components at any one instant *structure*. If observations indeed were made at instances, the more correct statement would be that backdrops are constructed with reference to particular structures, not states. At the organization level of human systems, inflows and outflows typically are measured at boundaries. Those objects are processes, which occur over time. Therefore, we use the term *state* to describe observations, recognizing that organizational observations almost always contain both structures and processes. They are observations of substates of the steady state of an organization.

Multiple observations must be made to determine differences among entities or changes in a single entity. A means to distinguish one observation from another is needed. In Chapter 4 we constructed variables to distinguish one state from another. Now we need to describe different observations, each of which may be described by values, variables, and entities. Klir (1985: 35) terms such higher-order dimensions *supporting variables,* to distinguish them from the basic variables observed, as discussed in Chapter 4. Supporting variables are constructed from individual observations of entities, whereas basic variables are constructed from individual observations of states.

Supporting variables are time, identity of entity, and location:

1. *Time.* Time is a fundamental dimension of the physical space-time continuum and partly identifies observations. Structures exist at certain instances. States, as we describe them in organizations, are observed to exist in certain minute periods, and events are examined in longer but limited periods. Time is needed for measuring such dimensions as duration, speed, rate, and acceleration.

2. *Identity of the concrete entity.* Because an observation concerns the state of a certain entity, that particular entity must be identified. Identification takes place by means of identifiers. For instance, typical identifiers of persons are name, social security number, signature, sex, height, color and amount of hair, appearance (photo), and special distinguishing marks, among other personal data.

3. *Location.* Because concrete entities occupy physical space, they locate at a given moment in a certain spot in three-dimensional space (Miller 1978: 9–11). Location therefore may be used for the identification of the entity instead of other identifiers. Location sometimes is expressed very exactly by means of longitude, latitude, and altitude, but in most cases it is conveyed by such vague expressions as "That lady over there is Mrs. McPherson."

Only two of the supporting variables are needed for an unambiguous specification. The third virtually always is determined by the other two (Figure 5.2).

	TIME T	LOCATION L	IDENTITY OF THE ENTITY I
TIME	= L + I	(+)	(+)
LOCATION	(+)	= T + I	(+)
IDENTITY	(+)	(+)	= T + L

NOTE: Backdrop supporting variables distinguish one observation from another. They are mutually defined by each other (e.g., identity by time and location.)

Figure 5.2
Backdrop Supporting Variables

For instance, the identity of an entity can be given by means of time and location (i.e., the observation concerns the particular entity located at time t_1 in location l_1). The time of the entity, in turn, is determined by location and identity (i.e., location is where entity E_1 is at location l_1). The last inference, however, does not always hold. The same entity may be located at different points of time or for longer periods of time at the same location. Any two of these backdrops will, however, suffice for the identification of an event.

In many cases, the use of identifiers is far more practical than location. For instance, it is rather awkward to specify the entity by the expression "the person located at time t_1 in location l_1." It is far simpler to give a name, as in "This gentleman is Mr. McPherson," and thereafter to use the name whenever referring to him.

CONCEPTUAL SPACE AND ABSTRACT ENTITIES

Events also can be composed of abstract concepts. Abstract entities have no mass and, therefore, do not locate anywhere specifically in physical space. Instead of mass, however, they have meaning. Instead of being in physical space, they are located in the conceptual space of some theoretical scheme.

The definitions of concepts provide location in this conceptual space similar to that provided by longitude, latitude, and altitude in physical space. The map of this conceptual space consists of variable and entity hierarchies, and the number of its dimensions (variables) therefore varies. Sometimes conceptual space is unidimensional, sometimes multidimensional and sometimes multi-multidimensional, always depending on the number of hierarchic levels by which it is defined.

CHARACTERIZATION OF A SOURCE SYSTEM

The identification of an observed source system may be formally described as follows:

$$P^a,\ E^b,\ C_1,\ l_1,\ t_1 = S_1$$

where

1. P refers to the variable observed,
2. a gives the location of the variable in theoretical, conceptual space (defines the variable),
3. E refers to the entity,
4. b gives the location of the entity in theoretical, conceptual space (defines the entity),
5. c gives the entity identity (is an identifier),
6. t_1 refers to the respective instant$_1$,
7. l_1 to the respective location, and
8. S_1 is the value of the observed state.

The above observation reads "The entity E_c which is interpreted as belonging to the theoretical category b, which entity locates in l_1, at instant t_1, has the state s_1, which is conceived of as a value of variable P^b, which is interpreted as belonging to theoretical category a."

Two kinds of backdrops are required: one for spatiotemporal space and the other for conceptual space. Time and location are backdrops in physical space, and membership and aggregate hierarchies locate variables and the entities in conceptual space.

ELEMENT OBSERVATION

A source system generally is composed of many elements. An element observation consists of one dimension (variable), its backdrop, and the value of its

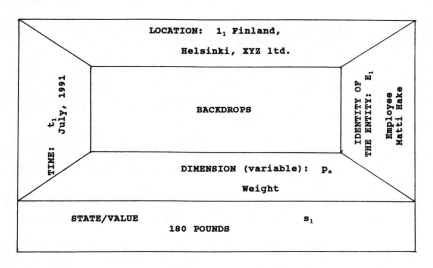

Figure 5.3
An Element Observation

state. Source systems are observed through their individual elements and the relations among them. The observation of an element is described in Figure 5.3. Its actual content is the value of a state s_1 (e.g., 180 pounds). It "belongs" to an entity E, with identity E_1 (e.g., person, named Matti Hake), who is located at time t_1 (July 1991) in location l_1 (Finland, Helsinki, XYZ ltd.). The identity of the entity E_1, location l_1, and time t_1 are physical backdrops of the element observation. The backdrops are expressed in the superscript of the symbol,

$$p^{backdrops} = s_1$$

If the states are organized, as they usually are, into variables, 180 pounds is conceived of as a value of the variable weight. If we observe Matti Hake as an employee, we categorize the entity E^b. Thus the content of an elementary observation has the form "The individual entity E_1 of category E^b, which is located in l_1 at time t_1, has, in the variable p^a, the value s_1."

DATA MATRIX—MULTIPLE-ELEMENT OBSERVATIONS

Multiple observations may be used to determine relations. Relations are identified by combining single observations in a manner that allows only one of the backdrops to change, the others being held constant. They are combined in order to determine the following relations (and, thus, processes):

1. Changes in time by combining the observations concerning the same variable and the same entity at different points of time (direction A in Figure 5.4). Identity and dimension are constant, meaning that the backdrop expands in the direction of time.

2. Differences among individual entities, averages for a population, and so on, by combining observations concerning the same variable and the same moment of time with reference to different entities. In this case, the identity varies in direction B.

3. A more holistic picture by combining observations concerning different variables of the same entity and at the same point of time (direction C).

In this way, the elementary observations are combined into three-dimensional data matrices. They are, however, presented in two dimensions with respect to

1. time and entity $(A + B)$ as in Figure 5.4, or
2. time and variable $(A + C)$, or
3. entity and variable $(B + C)$.

$-----> A$					
$t_1\ E_1\ p^a$ s_1	$t_2\ E_1\ p^a$ s_2	$t_3\ E_1\ p^a$ s_3	$t_4\ E_1\ p^a$ s_4	$t_5\ E_1\ p^a$ s_5	$t_6\ E_1\ p^a$ s_6
$t_1\ E_2\ p^a$ s_{11}				$t_5\ E_1\ p^b$ s_{14}	
$t_1\ E_3\ p^a$ s_{21}				$t_5\ E_1\ p^c$ s_{22}	
$t_1\ E_4\ p^a$ s_{61}				$t_5\ E_1\ p^d$ s_{31}	
$t_1\ E_5\ p^a$ s_{32}				$t_5\ E_1\ p^e$ s_{42}	
$t_1\ E_6\ p^a$ s_{41}				$t_5\ E_1\ p^f$ s_{58}	

NOTE: Combination of elementary observations either over time (direction A), over entities (B), or over dimensions (C).

Figure 5.4
Data Matrix Construction

July 1991	ENTITY EMPLOYEES OF COMPANY XYZ LTD.				
VARIABLES	EA	DA	CA	BA	...
Seniority	33 yrs	12 yrs	25 yrs	15 yrs	...
Bonus for seniority	20 %	10 %	20 %	15 %	...
Position	Executive manager	Manager	Middle manager	2nd Line supervisor	...
Job	"	Marketing manager	Technical manager	Superinten-dent in plant	...
Sex	Female	Male	Male	Male	...
Performance	Outstand-ing	Good	Good	Satis-factory	
...	...	...	...	...	...

NOTE: Individual elementary observations are combined into data matrices, in which the entities are in columns, the dimensions in rows and the states are where they intersect.

Figure 5.5
A Data Matrix

A data matrix may contain the following information for each individual entity (Figure 5.5):

Backdrop:
   Entity type: Employee of the firm XYZ ltd.
   Identity (name): EA, DA, CA, BA, and so forth.
   Time: July 1991, August 1991, September 1991, and so forth.

Observed variables:

   Seniority: 33 years, 12 years, and so forth.
   Bonus for seniority: 20 percent, 10 percent, and so forth.

The columns of such matrices represent entities, and the rows are the variables observed. The intersections of the columns and the rows are the values of the states of relevant entities in the respective variables. Source systems can be represented by tables of this kind. Of course, one table is required for each moment or period at which observations are made.

COEXISTENCE PAIR AND THE ELEMENTARY RELATION

One objective of scientific research is to find explanations for events or to predict them. This requires that possible dependencies between states, reasons for their existence, be located. Measurement procedures provide a strong means of comparing different states on a single variable. The complexity of organizations often requires that judgments be made based on information about more than a single variable. Identifying coexistence pairs moves a step beyond measurement to search for possible relationships among different variables.

This procedure begins by examining the states in pairs. A coexistence pair is formed when two different values of states of two different variables have the same backdrop. The states involved in a coexistence pair are partners. The connection between them is a relation or, to put it more precisely, a coexistence relation.

For instance, the observation "*FA,* who works as an office clerk, today receives a personal bonus of 5 percent and has served us for seven years" is such a pair (Figure 5.6). The partner states are "personal bonus of 5 percent" and "served us for seven years," and the connecting backdrop is "employee FA— during this study."

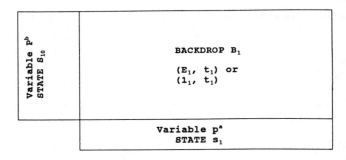

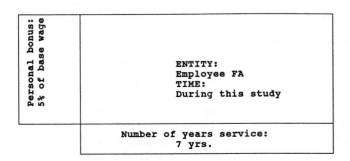

NOTE: A coexistence pair is formed when two states of two different variables have the same backdrop.

Figure 5.6
A Coexistence Pair

COEXISTENCE ROWS

In the search for associations between variables, the next step is to combine the individual pairs into compilations. This is possible if the pairs have a common backdrop that is wider than that of the original pairs. One typical compilation is a *row*. It is built up of two or more pairs having the same variables (dimensions) as their partners. Figure 5.7 provides an example of such a row: it concerns seniority and personal bonus. The first pair is the Figure 5.6 example of the employee, FA, with his seven years and 5 percent personal bonus. The other pairs give the same information regarding other employees, such as FB, FC, and FD. Although each other pair has a different individual backdrop, all the employees are in the service of the company XYZ ltd. We therefore are able to transfer the backdrop in an entity hierarchy from the individual level to the company level. There are actually two different backdrops: one is the connecting backdrop common to all of the pairs (which in Figure 5.7 is company XYZ ltd., 1991), and the other is what distinguishes the individual pairs from each other (which is employee in this case).

CONNECTING BACKDROP		DISTINGUISHING BACKDROP	ROW	
Time	Location	Entity Employees of XYZ ltd.	Seniority (yrs.)	Bonus (%)
1991	Company XYZ ltd.	FA	7	5
"	"	FB	0	0
"	"	FC	2	0
"	"	FD	4	0
"	"	FO	0	5
"	"	FU	2	10
"	"	FM	5	11
"	"	FE	10	10
"	"	FP	14	10
"	"	FT	8	16
...	...	...	...	...

NOTE: Combination of individual pairs into a row on condition that they have a common backdrop. In this case, they are all the employees of XYZ ltd. in 1991.

Figure 5.7
Combining Pairs into Rows

FROM ROWS TO COORDINATE SYSTEMS

A row is a rather impractical means of expression if the number of parts is large. It lacks a visual character. That difficulty can be overcome in most cases by presenting the rows in a two-dimensional, rectangular coordinate set. Each axis represents a partner variable of the row.

The abscissa of Figure 5.8 is seniority in years and the ordinate is personal bonus in percent of base wage. The individual pairs are placed on the grid formed by the scales of these axes. Thus, for instance, the employee FA of our example is in the square seven years, 5 percent.

When this has been done, one can sometimes see, purely with the naked eye certain regularities in the row. For instance, in Figure 5.8, all the pairs are in the upper half of the diagonal. More often, however, the eye is not a sufficient instrument to draw conclusions, and other more effective devices, such as mathematical methods, are needed.

GENERAL RULES

The regularities discovered by the naked eye or by mathematical methods are general principles followed by the set of pairs. In Figure 5.8, such a general rule seen at a glance is a seniority rule that may be stated as follows:

Service (Years)	Personal (Bonus $)
0< <5	0 or more
5< <10	5 or more
10< <15	10 or more
15< <20	15 or more
20<	20

Such generalizations are much more compact than the original verbal row of pairs and also more than that illustrated in Figure 5.7. They are, therefore, more economical with regard to space.

CONTINUATION OF THE ANALYSIS

The next stage of analysis draws attention to deviations from the primary generalized rule. In Figure 5.9, the deviation refers to all the personal bonuses that are greater than the bonuses entitled by the seniority rule, that is, to the notion "or more." The analysis is completed by "chasing" reasons for those deviations. In our example, the assumed explanation for the higher personal bonuses might be performance level. This is investigated by placing the devia-

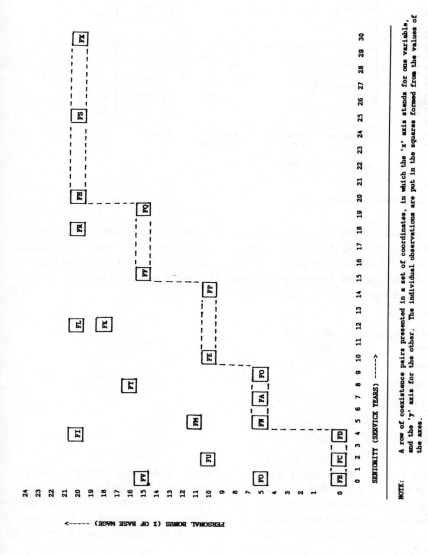

NOTE: A row of coexistence pairs presented in a set of coordinates, in which the 'x' axis stands for one variable,
         and the 'y' axis for the other. The individual observations are put in the squares formed from the values of
         the axes.

Figure 5.8
A Row of Coexistence Pairs on a Set of Coordinates

87

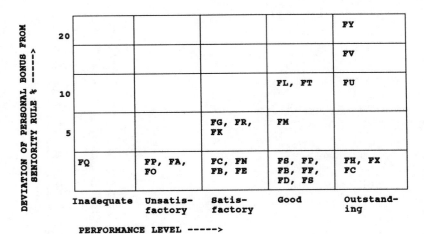

Figure 5.9
Deviations from Primary Rule

tions (personal bonus minus bonus identified by the seniority rule) in a new set of coordinates, with the abscissa indicating the performance level, and the ordinate indicating the deviation in percent of base wage. This has been done in Figure 5.9. All the cases are below the diagonal. The rule that can be inferred on this basis may be termed *merit bonus*. It reads:

Performance Level	Personal Bonus %
Inadequate	0
Unsatisfactory	0
Satisfactory	max. 5
Good	max. 10
Outstanding	max. 20 ·

From this point the analysis continues according to the same principle, meaning, in our example, that deviations from the merit rule are examined next (Figure 5.10). This entails asking the question why the merit bonus is lower than the maximum. The explanation for these deviations is assumed to be gender based. It is suspected that wage earners are being discriminated based upon sex. Sex will, therefore, be located on the abscissa, and deviation from the seniority rule on the ordinate (Figure 5.10). This shows that the personal bonus for women is based solely on the seniority rule, whereas for men it is based both on seniority

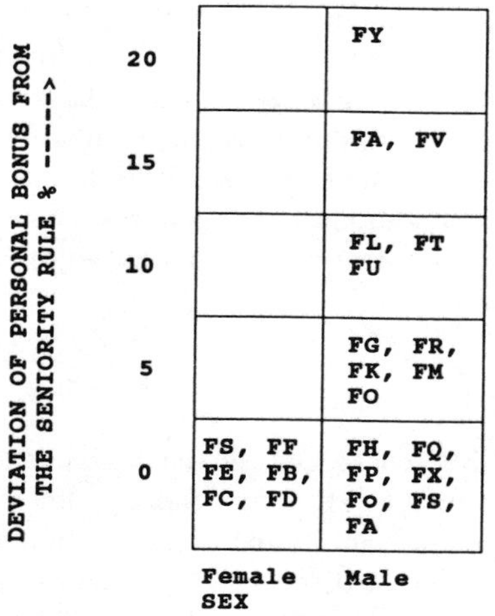

DEVIATION OF PERSONAL BONUS FROM THE SENIORITY RULE % ---->	Female	Male
20		FY
15		FA, FV
10		FL, FT FU
5		FG, FR, FK, FM FO
0	FS, FF FE, FB, FC, FD	FH, FQ, FP, FX, FO, FS, FA
	Female SEX	Male

NOTE: Deviations from the secondary rules are again subjected to further analysis and are compared with the suspected explanatory variable.

Figure 5.10
Investigating Higher-Level Generalized Rules

and merit bonus. The general rule that may be concluded from this observation, termed *gender bias,* is:

Sex	Personal Bonus
female	seniority bonus (no merit bonus)
male	seniority plus merit bonus

The analysis still may continue, because even the men's personal bonuses do not depend logically on seniority and performance level. Some male employees' personal bonuses are sums of seniority and performance bonuses. Other bonuses are not. Upon analysis, two new explanations may be found:

1. The sum may not exceed 20 percent, which is the maximum.
2. When the sum is lower than 20 percent, the deviation depends on the employee's superior. If a superior has not suggested a raise, an employee does not receive the merit bonus, even if he is otherwise entitled to it. The rules for personal bonuses for men take the form: the personal bonus is the sum of the seniority and the merit bonus, provided that the superior is willing to award the merit bonus or the sum does not exceed 20 percent.

This chapter thus far has provided procedures for combining observations to produce information that may not be apparent in the raw data. Individual observations are combined with each other into pairs by means of backdrops. This allows a more thorough examination of relations. Some regularities may be found for one single relation, such as the rule of pay seniority in the examples. When the exceptions are analyzed, conditions for validating the rule can be found. Each of the conditions uncovers a new dimension (variable), and thus a new relation emerges from the rule.

DISPARITY: DIFFERENCE OR CHANGE

The other side of regularity is difference. One of the fundamental human capacities, perhaps the most fundamental of all, is the capacity for recognizing differences. It is, in any case, an important ability in the formulation of variable scales, as discussed in Chapter 4. While a scale was being constructed, such questions were asked as, Can one use the comparative degree with reference to this dimension, or Which value represents the maximum and which one is the minimum in this variable? These questions use the capacity for recognizing differences to make distinctions among states instead of to analyze the states themselves.

A distinction can exist between the states of two different entities at a given moment of time. These disparities between entities normally are called differences. Another use of disparities is comparing the different states of one and the same entity at different instances. The resultant disparity indicates how the entity has changed during the period between these instances. It is, therefore, called *change*. The backdrops of disparity, consequently, consist of either two entities and one point of time, or one entity and two points of time.

DISPARITY QUOTIENT, DISPARITY PAIR

Disparities may be examined in coexistence pairs, if they have a common backdrop. The purpose of such an examination is to determine the ratio of change of one variable to change in another (Figure 5.11). This is a particularly important concept in mathematics, because it describes the slope of the line or curve representing the dependence between these two variables or, mathematically speaking, the first derivate. If the dependence is linear, the quotient gives the angle or regression coefficient of the (regression) line.

A disparity pair actually contains two value pairs. In Figure 5.11, they are the two pairs of values of variables x and y (4,2) and (5,3). The difference between the values of x (*de x*) is 1, and so, too, is the respective change in y (*de y*) from 2 to 3. The quotient (*de y/de x*) is thus $1/1 = 1.0$ which describes the slope. Because this quotient varies, or may vary, from one point to another, it has to be

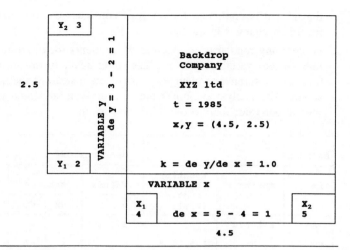

NOTE: A disparity pair is formed by two disparities, i.e. two pairs of the values of variables. It gives the slope, k, of the regression curve.

Figure 5.11
A Disparity Pair

specified or located with respect to the point that it represents on the curve. This is done by giving the middle point of both x values and both y values (4.5; 2.5), which means that the backdrop is widened. The identity of the entities and the moment of time is no longer sufficient. The backdrop must be completed with (x,y) coordinates of quotient, in our example 4.5; 2.5.

DISPARITY ROWS

When we look for dependence regularities between two variables, these disparity pairs or quotients at different points on the x,y coordinates must be compared. Sometimes it is easy to find this regularity, as in the example in Figure 5.12. The set of observations for (x,y) is (1,1), (2,2), (3,3), (4,4), and (5,5). The disparities between those pairs (dx,dy) are constant, i.e., (1,1) and the quotient is also therefore constant (1.0). This means that the dependence is linear.

By means of these quotients, the characteristics of the relevant dependence relation can be specified by questions like the following:

1. Is the ratio of change in the dependent variable to the corresponding change in its independent variable constant at all values of the independent variable? If the answer is yes, the dependence is linear; if no, it is non-

linear. If it is nonlinear, the analysis continues by formulating questions regarding changes in quotients.

2. Is there any regularity in changes of quotients for different values of the independent variable? The process starts again from the beginning, but now with reference to changes in quotients instead of the quotients themselves. The analyst examines the first derivate and then goes on to the second derivate, then to the third, and so on.

BACKDROP			OBSERVATIONS				
Time	Entity	Location Central Point (x,y)	Values		Changes		Ratio Quotient
			x	y	dx	dy	dy/dx
1985	XYZ ltd		1	1			
"	"	1.5, 1.5			1	1	1.0
"	"		2	2			
"	"	2.5, 2.5			1	1	1.0
"	"		3	3			
"	"	3.5, 3.5			1	1	1.0
"	"		4	4			
"	"	4.5, 4.5			1	1	1.0
"	"		5	5			
"	"	5.5, 5.5			1	1	1.0
"	"		6	6			

NOTE: Disparity pairs may be examined as "rows."   If the ratio dy/dx is constant over all values of x, the dependence is linear.

Figure 5.12
Disparity Rows

FROM COEXISTENCE TO CAUSAL RELATIONS

Up to this point this book has examined relations between values of states on the same and different variables. A regularity discovered in a coexistence relation actually means that the corresponding variables vary according to some general rule. These kinds of coexistence relations are termed *covariation relations,* if they exist between variables or state rows. In a verbal expression such as "whenever it rains, it's also cold," whenever stands for coexistence relation between values of states. The sentence "temperature varies in relation to cloudiness" may be interpreted as a covariation relation between variables.

Managers need to understand organizational processes from the point of view of causality. A coexistence relation between two states is causal if one of them is the reason for the existence of the other: one is the cause and the other is the effect. Such a causal relation between states is called a cause-and-effect-relation. A causal relation between variables and entities is an influence relation. Cause-and-effect and influence relations are common names for many concepts such as

- determinant, when it refers to something fixing the nature of results,
- dependence, when it means the quality of being influenced by another variable or entity,
- reason, when it expresses something that precedes and indicates an effect or result, or
- other expressions referring to a traceable and explainable cause of a known effect.

In everyday language, for instance, the sentence "his pay is high because he has served our company that long" is a pair of states linked by a cause-and-effect-relation. The word *because* is regarded as referring to such a relation. The sentence "bonus for seniority depends on service years" is a variable pair with an influence relation represented by the word *depends*.

SUMMARY

This chapter presented several procedures for using backdrops to discover relationships among the multiple observations of source systems. The initial procedures directly uncover regularities (commonalities) among observations. The later ones discover regularities in disparities. Both types are useful in managerial investigations.

REFERENCES

Klir, G. J. (1985). *Architecture of systems problem solving*. New York: Plenum Press.
Miller, J. G. (1978). *Living systems*. New York: McGraw-Hill.

6

The Big Picture: Combinations of Analysis Results

Until now, this book has focused mainly on analysis, on dividing a subject matter into values, variables, entities, and relations. The results of analysis have only limited utility unless they are combined into a general overview. Managers strive for a coherent picture of the phenomenon they manage. Constructing compilations and synthesizing results are natural sequels to analysis.

This chapter pulls together the combinative aspects of the methods already discussed and extends the discussion to more holistic combinations of management information. Whereas previous chapters have emphasized the connection of management information to concrete processes and raw information flows, this chapter focuses on higher-order connections as managers conceptualize very general (highly abstract) purposes and goals. It nevertheless starts at the bottom and moves up.

When dependencies or influence relations are presented by means of values, the smallest piece of information is a coexistence pair, such as "if a person has served less than five years, he doesn't get any seniority bonus" (no bonus ← less than 5 years) or "people, who have been in service more than twenty years receive a seniority bonus of 20 percent" (20 percent bonus ← more than 20 years).

Such pairs may be combined into coexistence rows, provided their value partners belong to the same variables as do the above sentences dealing with seniority and the respective bonus. They may, therefore, be combined into a row using the following rule.

Seniority bonus is based on seniority as follows:

Service Years	Seniority Bonus % of Base Wage
0< <5	0
5< <10	5

10< <15	10
15< <20	15
20<	20

In an analogous way, different coexistence rows of value pairs may be merged into a larger combination, if the rows have one variable in common. Such a compilation is termed a *value model,* as exemplified by Figure 6.1. It consists of

```
1.   Personal bonus depends on
               . seniority bonus,
               . merit bonus,
               . sex and
               . the opinion of the superior.

2.   Seniority bonus is based on seniority in the following way:

               SERVICE                  SENIORITY BONUS
               YEARS                    % OF BASE WAGE
                0< <5                          0
                5< <10                         5
               10< <15                        10
               15< <20                        15
               20<                            20

     Seniority bonus is paid unconditionally on the basis of
     service years.

3.   Merit bonus is based on performance level in the following
     way:

               PERFORMANCE              MERIT BONUS %
               LEVEL                    OF BASE WAGE
               Inadequate                       0
               Unsatisfactory                   0
               Satisfactory             <    5
                                        =
               Good                     <   10
                                        =
               Outstanding              <   20
                                        =

4.   The employee's superior decides the final amount of the
     merit bonus. He can pay lower bonuses but may never exceed
     the above rule.

5.1  The personal bonus of female employees is based solely on
     the seniority rule.

5.2  For male employees the personal bonus is:
     a) the sum of seniority bonus and merit bonus
     b) provided that
          ba) the superior recommends the payment of merit bonus
              and
          bb) the sum does not exceed 20 %
```

```
NOTE:  A value model is composed of coexistence rows, which consist
       of value pairs.  These results show a bias against women
       that is not apparent without analysis.
```

Figure 6.1
A Value Model

an initial rule that serves as a list of contents and enumerates all the rows included in the model. The first rule in Figure 6.1 cites the elements and bases for personal bonuses and thus constitutes a list of this kind. The model then presents all the rows and rules mentioned in the list.

VARIABLE MODELS

Each coexistence row of value pairs corresponds to a variable pair. It describes in considerable detail the interdependence of these variables and also can be presented by means of variables. The influence relation is symbolized by an arrow. The $+$ or $-$ signs beside the arrow denote the direction of changes, $+$ standing for parallel changes (y increases as x increases) and $-$ for the opposite tendency. If the dependence is known in the form of a row, it can be written beneath the independent variable as in Figure 6.2.

Such a variable pair also may be inferred directly from analysis; it consists of a statement such as "personal bonus depends on seniority" or "personal bonus depends on the wage earner's merits." These variable pairs represent the elemental information in variable language.

Variable pairs can be combined into a star, containing all the variables influencing one and the same dependent variable. This can be done if the variable pairs have one variable in common. The above two sentences, for instance, have personal bonus as a common variable. Together with other sentences dealing with personal bonus, they thus form the star in Figure 6.3. Again, describing the corresponding value rows makes the star more informative.

Different stars may in turn be combined into a larger compilation, provided they possess, pairwise, one common variable (Figure 6.4). This compilation is another form of a variable model.

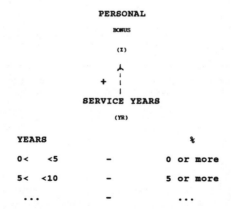

Figure 6.2
Variable Model

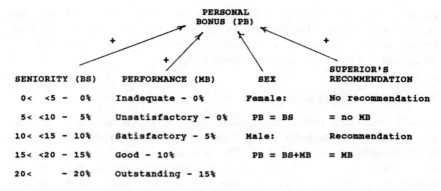

Figure 6.3
A Variable Star

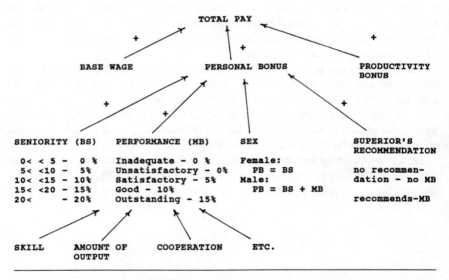

NOTE: Stars contain variable pairs consisting of two variables and an
         influence relation between them.

Figure 6.4
A Variable Model of Stars

ENTITY MODELS

Value and variable models can be transformed into entity models by presenting the entities described by values or by variables (Figure 6.5). Entity models
correspond to value models such as that of Figure 6.1. The respective variables
or values may be written in the entity model, as has been done in Figure 6.5.

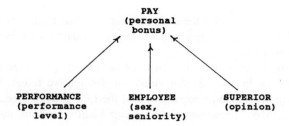

Figure 6.5
An Entity Model

An alternative is to trace the entities directly from the text. This process begins from entity pairs, expressed in such sentences as "pay depends on the wage-earner's performance" (pay ← performance), or "pay is also influenced by who the wage-earner is" (pay ← employee) or "superiors decide on how much is paid" (pay ← superior). Such entity pairs can be combined together into a star, as in Figure 6.5, provided they have one entity in common. These entity stars can be combined into a larger network—into an entity model—if the stars share certain entities. The process is quite similar to that involved in building variable models.

In this way, observations concerning dependencies between terms may be made at three levels:

1. at the entity level, explaining what things have an impact on each other,
2. at the variable level, explaining which variables are mutually dependent, and
3. at the value level, explaining how the variables depend on each other, or which values go together.

HIERARCHIES

Chapter 4 introduced the process by which values of variables are combined into part hierarchies, variables into membership hierarchies, and entities into part (aggregate) or membership hierarchies. Value, variable, and entity models are similar to those hierarchies. The difference is in the type of connections among the terms. The connections are influence or covariance relations in the models, and they are part or membership relations in the hierarchies.

In a part hierarchy, the element is a pair in which one term is part of another. For instance, the sentence "One Finmark is 100 pennies" states that a penni is part of a Finmark. Such pairs can be combined into stars (however, we term such stars *element hierarchies*) if they, pairwise, have terms in common.

The procedure is similar for constructing membership hierarchies. The element is a concept pair connected with a membership relation. Pairs are combined into element hierarchies, and these in turn are combined into an ordinary hierarchy, as in Figure 6.6. In this way elemental models easily become part of hierarchical constructs.

In Figure 6.6, the bases for distribution of welfare are presented in the form of a hierarchy. At the bottom are the values of distributive bases, the episodes, which in turn are combined into variables of the first order. These are combined into several element hierarchies, such as punctuality, working harmony, reliability, or initiative. The variables of the first order are then recombined into new element hierarchies, producing variables of the second order, such as quality, organizational climate, and flexibility. These form new element hierarchies that produce variables of the third order, such as economic efficiency, human efficiency, and performance level in the employee's main job. In this way, new element hierarchies are formed and combined with each other until all the concepts are under one and the same heading, which in this case is "distributive bases."

PRINCIPLES OF COMBINATION

This chapter summarizes how information regarding phenomena, dependencies, and cause-and-effect relations can be described holistically as models, and how concepts can be summarized in hierarchies. These are the combinational tools a systems theory offers its users.

Certain principles should be followed in the combination process. If we limit our examination to membership hierarchies and influence models (the most-used compilations), five principles apply. They are sufficient generality, common partner, common hierarchy, standardized meaning, and matching generality.

Sufficient Generality

Before it is possible to combine pairs, one must make sure that the pairs have sufficient generality, and that the regularity has a wide enough backdrop. The pair should have reasonable time generality (has existed long enough) and entity generality, (applies to a wide enough population). The pair should also have sufficient condition generality. If a piece of information is only valid subject to too many conditions, it will apply only on very special occasions and will, therefore, be far less useful than an unconditional piece of information. Where membership relations are concerned, this means that the definition must have wide enough acceptance among specialists and laypersons. As such, acceptance generality is more extensive, the thought constructs are more understandable and they find broader acceptance.

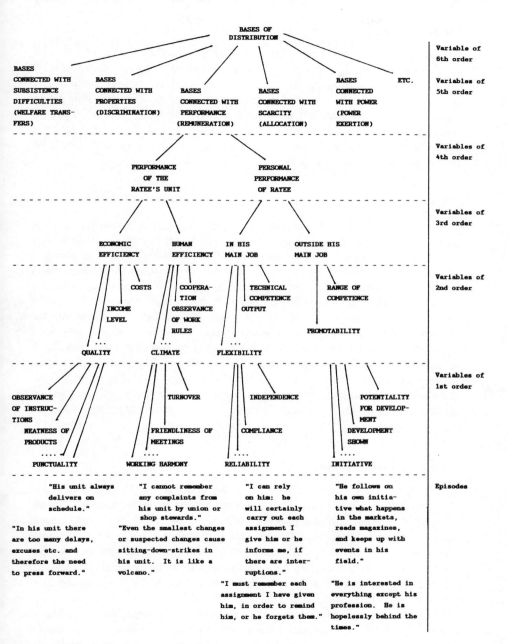

Figure 6.6
Distributive Bases as a Variable Hierarchy

101

Common Partner

Two membership pairs can be combined with each other if they have at least one partner in common. Hierarchies are constructed in this way. In the same way, two variable pairs possessing an influence relation can be combined into a star, and so can two entity pairs, if they have one partner in common. With value pairs, the cause-and-effect relation may be carried still further: the pairs can be combined into a chain of stars if they have only one variable in common, even if this is not the same value. In this way, one can move from pairs to stars, and from stars to hierarchies and networks.

Common Hierarchy

Pairs also may be combined, even if they do not have common partners but possess two concepts that are in the same hierarchy at different hierarchic levels, or at a different location on the same level. This also means that a regularity, a verified hypothesis, may be transferred from one level to another. For example, a law found to be true with regard to pay can be applied to resources and resource rewards, and even to welfare in general. This means that when pay differences motivate people's actions, so also do resource and welfare differences, on the assumption that the differences are logically tied to people's performance. Such regularities might also be transferred horizontally on the same hierarchic level; for instance, everything that holds good for pay also could be valid with respect to price formation. But it only *could* be. One must be careful in making these transfers. A true statement concerning one variable only entitles us to a question about another variable in the same hierarchy. Could what is true for pay also be true for prices?

Standardized Meaning

Only rarely do the same concepts have the same names. In those cases, and also if there is reason to believe that the same-concept name does not necessarily refer to the same concept, it is necessary to analyze the meanings of concepts and names assumed to possess the same meaning. But sometimes, even the original definitions offered by the literal sources are not similar, and the semantic components differ. It is then necessary to present both definitions by means of standardized defining concepts. If the standardized definitions are similar, then the pairs can be combined.

For making compilations, managers should complete concept cards similar to that of Figure 6.7. These cards contain the original definition of the relevant concept in the form it was acquired from the literature or from open-end questionnaires. They also contain the same definition in standardized form, estab-

Concept Name Originally C_1^{10}						
Standardized Name C_2^1						

Defining Variables						
Original Variable Name	p^{11}	p^{12}	p^3	.....	p^{13}	p^4	p^{14}
Standardized Name	p^1	p^2	p^3	.....	p^5	p^4	p^6
Original Value	p_1^{11}	p_3^{12}	p_3^3	.....	p_5^{13}	p_2^4	p_7^{14}
Standardized Value	p_2^1	p_1^2	p_1^3		p_4^5	p_2^4	p_7^6

Figure 6.7
A Concept Card

lished by means of terms taken from a particular conceptual frame. This principle is important in concrete process management for interpreting organizational information flows in terms of LST.

Such cards are compared with each other before making a combination. If the concept name is the same and the assumed meaning is also the same or if concepts with different names have a similar original definition, there is reason to believe that their standardized definitions are also the same. Also, if concepts with different names and different original definitions have the same standardized definition, they may be regarded as the same concept and thus used as criteria for the combination of pairs.

Matching Generality

When pairs are combined, their generality is seldom the same. In most cases, the time generality is sufficient for combination. However, some entity generalities may be so different that combining them would be invalid. Empirical research projects are typically narrow, and their results generally, therefore, apply to different populations. In such cases, when the results are combined one has to pay great attention to the environment in which the studies were performed.

If, for instance, one study rates pay as third in importance as a motivator and another places it in tenth place, one must analyze the number of competing motivators in each study. The type of pay system, to what extent pay depends on performance, influences results. This means that before different results can be combined, they should have approximately the same condition generality, and the person making the combinations, at least, should be aware of the differences in condition generality.

SUMMARY

This short chapter has summarized combinative ideas and aspects of L-M theory methods. Chapters 4, 5, and 6 provide examples of the fundamental methods and procedures of L-M theory. This theory and thus those methods and procedures are combined with LST to manage the concrete processes of organizations.

Every manager remembers mathematics and algebra courses. Few of us had great difficulty with the algebraic manipulations and algorithm performances. Those troublesome word problems were something else. Getting from the sentences to the formal organization of information is without doubt the more difficult aspect of this whole process.

Primarily for that reason, Chapters 7, 8 and 9 are devoted to introducing a number of different methods developed by different people in different settings for analyzing and synthesizing linguistic information into formal schemes. The different schemes are compared to the L-M theory concepts introduced throughout Chapters 4, 5, and 6.

A secondary, but important, reason for Chapters 7, 8 and 9 is that this book, although very pragmatic, is not a step-by-step how-to manual. It concerns applied theory and provides many examples as a means of conveying the idea of that theory to managers. Most important, a philosophy of management is introduced that connects our best ideals with organizational behavior. The strong emphasis on applications is to communicate that philosophy, and to demonstrate that it can be applied practically.

7

Syntactic Analysis
and Its Methods

This and the following two chapters introduce several different methods of analyzing and synthesizing linguistic information. This chapter concerns syntactic methods, and the next two focus on semantic methods.

Different methods may be used more easily in different organizations depending on already existing mind sets. The mind sets of some organizations are more quantitative than those of others. Some managers are process oriented, while others are structure oriented.

Syntactic analyses provide procedures for examining and combining observational information to assess the purposes of organizations as expressed in their communications flows. They are particularly useful for identifying relations among terms. Semantic methods alternatively focus on terms.

METHODOLOGY
OF CONTENT ANALYSIS

A qualitatively oriented systems theory should provide its users with certain devices for analyzing the content of linguistic communications. Two kinds of linguistic information should be analyzed.

One describes events and phenomena by means of concepts. This kind of information is presented in propositions, describing how things are. Propositions are either factual statements, denoting the actual or existing occurrence of different states, or value statements, attributing evaluations of the states described, such as good or evil, desirable or undesirable, right or wrong, or the existence of rights or obligations. The statements thus denote either how things are or how acceptable they are. The analysis of these propositions is termed *syntactic operations*.

The other kind of verbal information consists of definitions describing what is meant by the concepts used in propositions. Before the message of a proposition can be understood fully, the definitions of its concepts should be analyzed, and heterogeneous names and definitions should be standardized and organized into hierarchies. These actions are examples of semantic operations.

Content analysis methodology consists of instructions on how to accomplish both of these operations. Thus, content analysis is bipartite. Semantic methods show how to analyze and construct definitions and how to build up hierarchies. Syntactic methods, in turn, indicate in what way statements can be analyzed or constructed, and how compilations can be built up from individual statements. These instructions provide a means of connecting systems theory directly to any kind of linguistic text.

SYNTACTICS

The term *syntactics* has at least two different meanings. According to the narrower linguistic definition, it is the branch of linguistics dealing with the syntax of natural languages, with grammatical rules describing how sentences and clauses are constructed with words and phrases. Syntactics, in its broader application, studies the formal relations of signs and expressions in general, not merely in the linguistic sense. We use the terms syntactics and syntactical in the broader sense.

Syntactical theories thus recognize constituent structure—the way words and phrases form statements of different dimensions. Conversely, a syntactic theory offers a method by which verbal expressions may be divided into parts, and by which these parts can be connected with each other. A syntactic theory thus always possesses two distinctly different functions: an analytical one and a synthetical one. A synthetical function constructs statements, and an analytical function divides clauses and sentences into different kinds of elements. We examine syntactics from the perspective of each of these functions.

LINGUISTIC-MATHEMATICAL METHOD
OF CONTENT ANALYSIS

Before surveying the various methods of content analysis that may be regarded as syntactical, the L-M theory approach is summarized. Following the summary, methods representative not only of general linguistics but also of other disciplines in the behavioral sciences, such as political science, psychology, and jurisprudence, will be reviewed. They are discussed briefly and compared with the L-M theory approach.

The L-M theory method proceeds in steps as follows:

1. *Interpretation* is the step of splitting the text into different kinds of logico-

mathematical terms and relations. A sample text: This man's pay is good and so he's fairly well motivated to work. Interpretation:

> this man = term = entity
>
> (amount of) pay = term = variable
>
> good = term = value of the preceding variable
>
> therefore = relation = cause-and-effect relation
>
> he (this man) = term = entity
>
> fairly well motivated to work = term = value
>
> (motivation = term respective variable)

This phase is actually the function referred to in the name of the method (linguistic-mathematical). The linguistic and other verbal concepts are translated into logico-mathematical ones.

2. *Formal presentation* describes the content of the analyzed text by means of the interpreted concepts. The above example continues in formal presentation: "The variable 'pay' of the entity 'this man' has the value 'good.' It is the cause. The effect is that the variable 'motivation' of the entity 'this man' has the value 'fairly well motivated' " or "pay $^{\text{this man}}$ = good $\rightarrow$ motivation $^{\text{this man}}$ = fairly well motivated."

3. *Combination* combines the results of analysis into pairs, stars, and models as introduced in the previous chapters.

One additional and essential feature in this approach is that it employs three different languages: they are propositions presented in entity, variable, value languages, or any combination of them. The methods described in the following sections are compared with this method and examined for the analytical steps they employ.

COMPARISON WITH LINGUISTIC-MATHEMATICAL PRINCIPLES

The syntactical principles of our systems theory, as summarized in Figure 7.1, employ two kinds of hierarchies. One of these is the hierarchy of systems theory concepts, according to which concepts are divided into terms and relations. Terms are divided into values, variables, and entities, and relations are divided into different types (Figure 7.2).

This theory hierarchy suggests several questions: Without dividing them into subcategories, with what kind of terms does the method introduced operate? Does it operate with values, variables, and/or entities? With what kind of relations does it operate?

LANGUAGE	TERM LANGUAGE Operates with terms and relations between them	VALUE LANGUAGE Operates with values and relations between them	VARIABLE LANGUAGE Operates with variables and relations between them	ENTITY LANGUAGE Operates with entities and relations between them
SIZE OF BODY OF INFORMATION				
MODELS	TERM MODEL	VALUE MODEL	VARIABLE MODEL	ENTITY MODEL

(COMPILATIONS OF SECOND ORDER) Contain two or more compilations of first order	$T^1 \leftarrow T^2 \leftarrow T^3$ $\uparrow$ T^4 T^5 $\uparrow \nwarrow$ T^6 T^7	1. $p^a = p^a + p^c$
		 2. $p^a \leftarrow p^b$
		    1 2
		 $p^a \leftarrow p^b$
		   2 2
		 $p^a \leftarrow p^b$
		   3 3
		 3. $p^c \leftarrow p^d$
		    1 1
		 ... ...
			$p^a \leftarrow p^a \leftarrow p^b$ $\uparrow \nwarrow$ p^c p^f $\uparrow \nwarrow$ p^d p^g	$E^1 \leftarrow E^2 \leftarrow E^3$ $\uparrow$ E^4 E^5 $\nwarrow$ E^6 E^7

COMPILATIONS OF FIRST ORDER Contain two or more pairs	CHAIN, STAR $T^1 \leftarrow T^2 \leftarrow T^3$ T^1 T^4 T^4 $\uparrow \nwarrow$ T^6 T^7	ROW $p^a \leftarrow p^b$ 1 1 $p^a \leftarrow p^b$ 2 2 $p^a \leftarrow p^b$ 3 3	CHAIN, STAR $p^a \leftarrow p^a \leftarrow p^b$ p^a p^c p^c p^d p^g	CHAIN, STAR $E^1 \leftarrow E^2 \leftarrow E^3$ E^1 E^4 E^4 $\uparrow \nwarrow$ E^6 E^8

PAIR Contains two terms & coexistence or influence relation between them	TERM PAIR Term T^2 is influenced by or exists with term T^3 $T^2 \leftarrow T^3$	VALUES PAIR The value p^a is
		         1
		 the effect and the value p^b is
		         1
		 the cause $p^a \leftarrow p^b$
		 1 1
			VARIABLE PAIR The value of variable p^a depends on the value of variable p^b
			
			 $p^a \leftarrow p^b$
				ENTITY PAIR Entity E^3 affects entity E^2.
				
				 $E^3 \leftarrow E^2$

ELEMENT STATEMENT Gives one state quality or identity of a term	Term T^1 belongs to terms T^2 $T^x = T^2$
	      1
		Entity E has in variable p^a the value p^a
		       1
		 $p^{aE} = p^a$
		         1
			Entity E has variable p^a
			
			 p^{aE}
				Entity E^1 belongs to entities E^1
				
				 $E^x = E^1$
				       1

NOTE: A syntactic method may operate with term language or with value, variable, and/or entity language. Analytical methods divide text into element statements and the latter into concepts. Synthetical methods combine the analysis results into compilations of different sizes.

Figure 7.1
Syntactic Method of L-M Theory

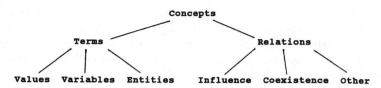

Figure 7.2
Hierarchy of Systems Theory Concepts

The other hierarchy deals with the size of statements. According to the L-M theory view, one may combine element statements into pairs, and pairs into rows, chains, stars and other compilations of the first order, and combine these in turn into models, networks, and other types of compilations of the second order (Figure 7.3).

This hierarchy suggests a second set of questions. This set is focused on the synthetic approach of the method. Does the process provide a method allowing the results of analysis to be combined into compilations? If so, what kinds of compilations?

These two hierarchies and their corresponding sets of questions will be compared with the procedures employed by other syntactical methods. Those methods are introduced next.

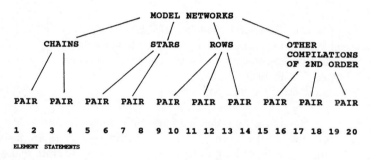

Figure 7.3
Compilations Hierarchy

SYNTACTIC METHODS INTRODUCED

The selection of methods is not intended to be exhaustive but is intended to illustrate different approaches by example. The methods have been chosen based on the following: they must show how verbal expressions are divided into parts corresponding to linguistic, logical, or other kinds of concepts, and they must pay attention to relations and other connections between the parts.

In the literature dealing with content analysis, methods of this kind are not always described as syntactical. For example, Krippendorf uses the term *discursive,* referring to formal, orderly, and normally extended expressions of thoughts on a subject (1969). We, however, have used the term *syntactical,* because its use is more widespread.

The methods may be classified into four main categories, according to the theoretical schemes by which they examine the structure of verbal expressions. The classification takes the following form:

I. Linguistic methods (operating with linguistic terms)
   A. Syntactic (linguistic) analysis
   B. Syntactic graphs
   C. Semantic or cognitive networks
   D. Linked member tables
II. Methods based on proposition calculus
   A. Proposition calculus
   B. Discursive content analysis
   C. N-SIM-method
   D. Picturing method
III. Methods based on the theory of graphs
   A. Signed diagraph technique
   B. Cognitive mapping
   C. Psychologic
   D. Interpretative Structural Modeling (ISM)
IV. Associative methods (concentrating on coexistence relations)
   A. Coordinative method for social policy target programs
   B. Contingency analysis
   C. Evaluative assertion analysis

Some of these methods are introduced briefly and compared with L-M theory, with special reference to the kinds of terms they employ. Others are just referenced. The purpose for presenting different methods is to illustrate that a wide variety of syntactic methods are available, not to provide detailed instruction on their use.

LINGUISTIC SYNTACTIC ANALYSIS

Conventional syntactic theories in linguistics usually are based on the idea that any expression of a natural language can be presented as a particular arrangement of elements corresponding to words or parts of sentences and possessing names that express their grammatical function. According to this procedure, the text subjected to syntactic analysis is divided into sentences; the sentences are divided into main and subordinate clauses (see Figure 7.4); the clauses are

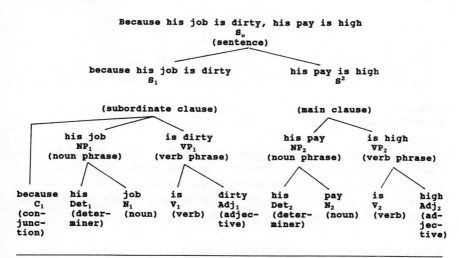

NOTE: Linguistic syntactic analysis divides sentences into linguistic elements and expresses their contents by tree diagrams.

Figure 7.4
Linguistic Syntactic Analysis

divided into noun and predicate phrases; the noun phrases are divided into nouns and determiners; and the predicate phrases are divided into verbs and auxiliaries (Lyons 1972). After sentences have been divided into elements in this way, they are represented by tree diagrams, as in Figure 7.4.

This type of linguistic analysis compares with the L-M theory approach in the following ways: adjectives (dirty, high) correspond to the values of variables, nouns (job, pay) to the entities, and conjunction (because) to a cause-and-effect relation. The syntactic tree resembles the concept hierarchies. A sentence is divided into smaller and smaller parts until the elementary parts are reached.

SYNTACTIC GRAPHS

Another lesser-known linguistic syntactic method is the technique of syntactic graphs, developed in Czechoslovakia by Klir and Valach (1967). According to this method, a sentence is regarded as consisting of phrases called *sentence elements*. Sentence elements form syntactic pairs. In each pair, one element is always the main element and the other the dependent one. Graphs are constructed by representing syntactic pairs by means of arrows. Relations among elements are expressed by interrogative words, such as *what kind of, how,* or *where.*

The sample sentence in Figure 7.4 takes the form of the syntactic graph shown in Figure 7.5.

When this method is compared with our systems theory, the sentence elements

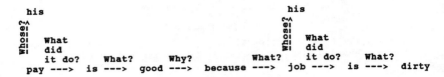

Figure 7.5
Syntactic Graph

correspond to terms. Syntactic graphs thus operate in terms, without being divided into entities, variables, values, or other subcategories. Analogously, there is only one category of relations symbolized by arrows, provided that one does not regard the interrogative words as representing subcategories of relations. The syntactic graph itself may be interpreted as a term model.

SEMANTIC OR COGNITIVE NETWORKS

Text linguistics is a branch of general linguistics that has developed the principle of dividing texts into units larger than single sentences. These larger units are termed *text sequences*. The method by which the content of sequences is examined is called the technique of semantic or cognitive networks (Sigurd 1974). An example of such a network is shown in Figure 7.6. With the help of this network, one can build up sentences varying in content by following the paths from various starting points. For example:

1. William, thirty years of age, lives in London.
2. Mary, age nineteen, works in a research group located in London.
3. William owns a car, driven by Lily, age twenty.
4. William knows Mary.
5. William, Lily, and Mary live in London.
6. Lily's colleague Peter, age forty, was vacationing in Rhodes.

These networks operate with various linguistic terms, analogous to different concepts in systems theory, for example:

1. Nouns such as "man," "woman," and "car" correspond to entities.
2. Nouns such as "name" or "age" are variables.
3. Numerals and nouns such as "thirty" and "William" are the values of variables.
4. Lines sometimes stand for a "belonging" relation, as in the "variable 'age' belongs to 'man' " and sometimes for influence relations, such as "knows" or "drives."

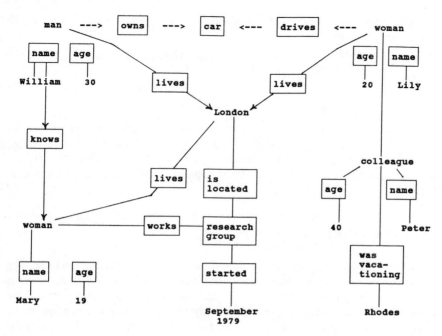

Figure 7.6
Semantic or Cognitive Network

The whole network may be seen as a term model, if it is studied as a network of nouns, verbs, numerals, or adjectives, together with their mutual connections. Some of its parts may be seen as element statements of the information concerning William (Figure 7.7). The diagram in Figure 7.7 reads: entity "man" has the value "William" in the variable "name" and value "thirty" in the variable "age." Or it reads: the entity E of quality "man" with the identity "William" has, for the variable "age," the value "thirty."

The content of a semantic network also can be interpreted partly as a descrip-

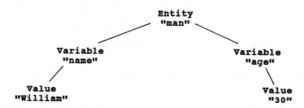

Figure 7.7
Element Hierarchy Concerning William

tive definition. For instance, the "man in the top, left-hand corner" in Figure 7.6 is specified as follows:

$$\begin{matrix} \text{man in} \\ \text{top} \\ \text{left} \\ \text{corner} \end{matrix} \quad \text{def) man \&} \quad \begin{matrix} 30 \text{ years} \\ \text{of age} \end{matrix} \quad \& \quad \begin{matrix} \text{by name} \\ \text{William} \end{matrix} \quad \& \quad \begin{matrix} \text{lives} \\ \text{in} \\ \text{London} \end{matrix} \quad \& \quad \begin{matrix} \text{knows} \\ \text{Mary} \end{matrix} \quad \& \quad \begin{matrix} \text{owns} \\ \text{a car} \end{matrix} \quad ($$

The semantic networks method thus describes the structure of sequences by means of their parts (words) and their mutual relations. It is, therefore, a syntactic method operating with term language. But it also provides definitions, hence, it is not a purely syntactic method, but a combination of syntactic and semantic methods.

TABLE OF LINKED ELEMENTS

Another aspect of interest to text linguistics is the plot of text sequences. The plot is the way new information emerges in a text. A table of linked elements is used to describe a plot. The text sequences are divided into parts, which are known as elements, and the linkages among the elements are described in the form of a table. An example is given in Figure 7.8. It describes the plot of the following story (Enkvist 1975):

1a. Once upon a time there was a king (b) who had a daughter.

2a. The king promised his daughter to whoever (b) brought him the strangest thing in the world.

3. There were then three boys living in a cottage.

4. The boys went in search of strange things.

5. They happened suddenly to find a snake that could go for miles with just a couple of bounces.

6. Immediately, the boys got hold of the snake.

7. The boys took the snake to the king's castle.

8. The king thought the snake was the strangest thing in the world.

9. The king gave his daughter to the eldest boy.

10. The other boys received large rewards (Enkvist 1975).

According to this method, the analyst isolates linked elements and then builds a matrix by allotting the elements to horizontal rows. Sentences and clauses are in vertical rows, and plus signs indicate links by showing the existence of a particular member in more than one sentence. In this example, for instance, the

ELEMENTS	SENTENCES										
	1a	1b	2a	2b	3	4	5	6	7	8	9	10
King	+	+	+						+	+	+	+
Daughter		+	+	+						+		
The one who brings the strangest thing in the world				+								
The strangest thing in the world				+		+			+			
Boys					+	+	+	+	+		+	+
A snake that could go for miles with just a couple of bounces							+	+	+	+		
Eldest boy											+	
Other boys												+
Great reward												+

Figure 7.8
Table of Linked Elements

king makes his appearance at the beginning and at the end of the story, and the boys in sentences three to seven and nine to ten. The reference to the king thus begins the story, the boys emerge in the middle, and both the king and the boys participate in the final scene.

According to the terminology of L-M theory, a matrix of linked members is an obvious entity model, because the linked members such as the king and the boys may be regarded as entities. The plus signs refer to the coexistence of entities, that is, to entity pairs or triplets. Thus, the matrix is an orthodox entity model, comprising not only influence relations, but all kinds of coexistence relations between the entities.

PROPOSITION CALCULUS

Even if this sounds unconventional, the proposition calculus of the discipline of logic may be interpreted as a syntactic method. It divides the text into parts and concentrates on the relations between these parts. It thus fits the definition of syntactic methods we formulated at the beginning of this chapter.

Proposition calculus examines the text as a combination of propositions formed from different kinds of terms. Among these terms, the following four may be mentioned as most relevant to content analysis: entities, properties of entities, relations between entities and/or properties, elementary propositions.

The propositions have different contents such as:

1. entity a has property P, i.e., $P(a)$
2. between entities a and b is relation R, i.e., $R(a,b)$,
3. between property P_i of entity a and property P_j of entity b is relation R, i.e., $R(P_i(a),P_j(b))$ or
4. if a, then b, i.e., $a \rightarrow b$.

With proposition calculus, the content is divided into parts corresponding to the terms of proposition calculus and then expressed by means of these terms (Pietilä 1975). We exemplify this procedure by means of the following three sentences:

1. His pay is high, because his job is dirty.
   Concepts:
   pay $=$ entity a
   high $=$ property p^1
   job $=$ entity b
   because $=$ implication $\rightarrow$
   Content:
   Dirty (job) $\rightarrow$ high (pay) or
   $P_2(b) \rightarrow P_1(a)$.
2. The level of pay depends on the dirtiness of the job.
   Concepts:
   wage level $=$ entity c
   dirtiness of job $=$ entity d
   depends $=$ dependence $=$ relation R^1
   Content:
   Dependence (wage level, dirtiness) or
   R_1 (c,d)
3. Job conditions influence wages.
   Concepts:
   job conditions $=$ entity e
   wage $=$ entity a
   influence $=$ influence relation $=$ relation R_2
   Content:
   Influence (job conditions, wage) or
   R_2 (e,a)

The correspondence of the terms of proposition calculus to the concepts of L-M theory is fairly clear, even if it is, to some extent, an alternative process. For example: properties (high, dirty) correspond to the values of variables; entities correspond, in some cases, to variables (dirtiness, level of pay), to the entities (pay, working conditions, job), and to relations to influence relations (because, depends, influences).

Accordingly, it is typical of proposition calculus that it operates with two of the three term categories of the L-M theory: entities and properties (values of variables). Hence, it pays implicit attention to entity and value language. It does not exclude variable language but translates it immediately into entity language.

DISCURSIVE CONTENT ANALYSIS

The technique of discursive analysis developed by Krippendorf obviously is based on proposition calculus (1969). Pietilä's study of the reception of the Finnish television program "Kolkhoz in Eastern Siberia" is a good example of its application (1975).

NORMALIZED SENTENCE-INDEX MATRIX
OR N-SIM-TECHNIQUE

Allen developed a method of content analysis for jurisprudence called *normalized sentence-index matrix,* or N-SIM technique (1965). Its purpose is to draft complicated statutes and decisions of the court in an accurate and intelligible way. It can be applied both manually and by computer.

The method is based on proposition calculus. The basic idea is to extract from the text all parts that can be transformed into normal sentences. Normal sentences are either "if and only if" or "if . . . then" sentences. The text is divided into elementary sentences, such as "the pitcher is careless" or "a spectator gets hurt" and then into syntax words that are either connectors or cause-and-effect relations. The content is expressed in the form of a network termed the normalized sentence-index matrix, in which sentences are symbolized by a capital S with a subindex, and syntax words by different kinds of lines. The N-SIM technique works as illustrated in Figure 7.9.

According to the terminology of L-M theory, the N-SIM matrices are orthodox value models, if we regard the sentences as descriptions of values of variables. The syntax words are either connectors, auxiliary concepts, or cause-and-effect relations. These matrices are thus value models consisting of values and cause-and-effect relations.

PICTURING METHOD

Carter developed a method for the visualization of content that he calls the picture or picturing method, PIX method (1975). It is based on proposition calculus and uses symbols to represent elements of communications.

```
        "If the pitcher is careless and a spectator gets hurt
or property is damaged, he is under obligation to indemnify
the victim for this injury or damage."
```

CONCEPTS

```
            "pitcher is careless" = sentence S₁

            "spectator gets hurt" = sentence S₂

            "property is damaged" = sentence S₃

            "pitcher is under obligation to indemnify the

victim for the injury or damage" = sentence S₄

            "if..., (then)" = syntax word >--->

            "and" = syntax word -----

            "or" = syntax word -----
```

CONTENT

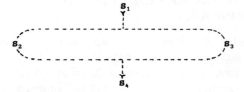

Figure 7.9
N-SIM-Method

SIGNED DIGRAPH TECHNIQUE

Roberts, among others, uses the ideas of graph theory to study complicated phenomena (1971). The basic concepts of the signed digraph technique are variables and their mutual influence relations. A text is interpreted and divided into variables and the influence relations among them. After individual sentences have been analyzed, the results are combined into networks. These normally are similar to the variable model of L-M theory. The nodes stand for variables, and the links (symbolized by arrows) describe influence relations. An example of such a signed digraph is provided by Figure 7.10, which represents a wage contract in which compensations for seniority, working conditions, and shift work are included. These paragraphs of the contract are conceived of as influence relations, because they show how pay depends on seniority and so on.

The technique of signed digraphs corresponds precisely to that of variable models. Each of them emphasize variables and influence relations, and each one builds up networks in a similar way. The idea of the variable model in our

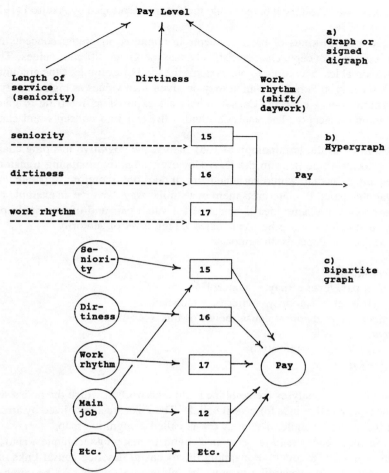

Figure 7.10
Examples of Graphs

systems theory has frankly been adopted, more or less consciously, from graph theory.

COGNITIVE MAPPING

Cognitive mapping is another method of content analysis based on the theory of graphs. It has been applied to research, for example, in political science and economics. We introduce it here mainly in the form developed by Axelrod (1976) and Hart (1976).

There are two kinds of basic concepts in cognitive mapping: concepts and causal beliefs. Concepts characteristically may be given different values. They are thus variables, according to our systems theory. For example, "the amount of British security in Persia"—which may be given such values as high security or low security—is a concept. Causal beliefs are expressions referring to causal links among concepts. The analysis divides the text into concepts and causal links.

According to the terminology of L-M theory, the cognitive mapping analyst tries to locate value pairs in the text. However, cognitive mapping transforms value pairs immediately into variable pairs. It does not, therefore, separate value and variable pairs, but interprets them in a similar way. We give an example here that expresses the same idea by means of a value pair and of a variable pair:

His pay is high, since he has reached a high level of seniority.

Level of pay depends on seniority.

Interpretation:

high pay, level of pay = concept *A*

high level of seniority, seniority = concept *B*

since, depends on = causal belief or link ←

Content:

wage level ← seniority or

$A \leftarrow B$.

The results of analyses are combined into a network in which the nodes stand for concepts and the links for causal beliefs. The links are symbolized by arrows, as in the above example. This network is called a cognitive map.

Different researchers have developed cognitive mapping techniques. Hart, for instance, has given cognitive mapping the means to describe causal links more thoroughly (1976). According to him, the following symbols may be combined with arrows for causal beliefs:

1. Plus or minus signs, referring to a dependence in which one party continuously increases or decreases, along with the increase of the other party.

2. If dependence first rises and then declines, Hart calls it "concave downward," denoted by the symbol *cd*. For instance:

Pace of	cd	Stability
economic	→	of social
growth		development

3. If the dependence first declines and then rises, Hart calls it "concave upward," denoted by the symbol *cu*.

4. If a causal link is undetermined (stochastic, for example), Hart calls it ambiguous and refers to it by the symbol *a*.

5. If there is no causal link between two concepts, it is termed *concept listing,* symbolized by 0 above the respective arrow.

A cognitive map is an orthodox variable model in our terminology. The meaning of the concept fits the definition of variable by comprising alternative and mutually exclusive values, and the causal links resemble the influence relations between variables.

PSYCHOLOGIC

Abelson and Rosenberg developed a method for the description of human cognitive processes termed *psychologic* (1958). It operates, on the one hand, with "thinglike" concepts referring to properties relevant in some way to the person and issue being studied, and, on the other hand, with "desirability relations" among thinglike concepts. A text is divided into thinglike concepts and desirability relations. For instance, the expression

wage → wage earner

reads "a wage is desirable for the wage earner." In this way, the results may be combined into networks, in which the nodes represent the thinglike concepts and the links stand for desirability relations, symbolized by arrows. Plus and minus signs express whether the concept is desirable or undesirable, respectively.

The thinglike concepts are obviously entities. The psychologic networks are thus entity models. Desirability relations may be conceived of as influence relations, perhaps more precisely as cost-benefit relations.

INTERPRETATIVE STRUCTURAL MODELING (ISM)

Interpretative structural modeling (ISM) is a tool for identifying a structure within a system. It was introduced by Farris and Sage (1975). The advantage of the method is that it transforms unclear or poorly articulated mental ideas into visible, well-defined models (Warfield 1976). It can be applied to any system containing identifiable elements related to each other in some fashion. Farris and Sage have, for instance, applied it to worth assessment, that is, a technique for determining the measure of desirability of a set of alternatives, when these alternatives are described by a multitude of attributes. The measure of worth is used as an element in the decision-making process for choosing among alternatives.

The basis of ISM is to be found in set and graph theory according to Warfield. Using ISM, the text to be analyzed is first divided into elements such as "convenient, accessible library facilities," "proximity to users," and "interlibrary system," and into different kinds of relations, the nature of which is determined by the interests of the analyst. Thus, Farris and Sage defined them as connections between two elements in which one is intended by the other, included within the meaning of the other, or an integral part of the other. In other words, the elements are examined on a pair-type basis with reference to some relation. The pairs are then organized into structural models by means of matrices and networks. In these networks, the nodes stand for the elements, and the links, either with or without arrow heads, for the relations.

According to L-M theory, ISM models may be regarded either as entity models, if the elements are entitylike concepts, or as variable models, if the elements emphasize attributes.

COORDINATIVE METHOD FOR SOCIAL POLICY TARGET PROGRAMS

Osmo Kuusi developed a method of content analysis for the coordination of the different administrative units or ministries of the Finnish state (1978). This method, which he calls a "coordinative method for social policy target programmes," is chiefly relevant to syntactic methods, even though it contains some clearly semantic constituents.

The recorded unit is either a target sentence or a means sentence. Target sentences have the general form "development is assumed to be such that x will be achieved," and means sentences read "measure y should be taken in order to achieve x state of affairs." "State x" is conceived of as a target and "measure y" as a means.

The target and means sentences are then analyzed in order to discover what kinds of targets and means have been specified in the various state administrative programs, and what kinds of dependencies have been mentioned between targets and means. These dependence relations, known as links, are located directly from the text or, if that is not possible, by making inferences.

An example of a sentence containing all three of these concept categories is the following:

The development of working conditions is necessary for the maintenance of the ability to work.

Concepts:

> development of working conditions = means sentence, $M1$
> maintenance of ability to work = target sentence, $T1$
> is necessary for = link $-----------$

Content:

development	maintenance
of working $-----------$	of ability
conditions	to work

> $M1$ $T1$

The targets found in the analysis are organized into main targets and sub-targets. They are then presented in the form of relevance trees or end hierarchies, according to their mutual links. By means of such an end tree, one can estimate which subtargets lead to which supertargets. The top half of Figure 7.11 is the

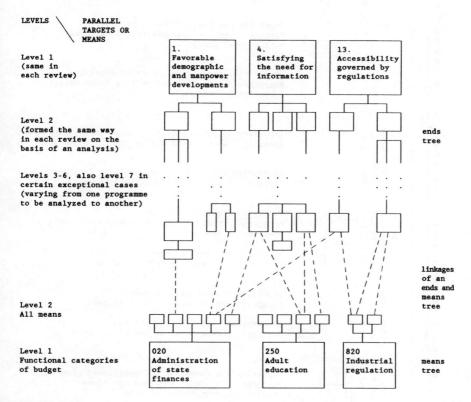

Figure 7.11
Coordinative Method for Social Policy Target Programs

schematic representation of such an end tree. In an analogous way, the means sentences are organized into a means tree, as exemplified by the bottom half of Figure 7.11. The relevant trees may be further developed into the form of a weighted tree, as in Figure 7.12, if the importance of the various parts are indicated in percentages.

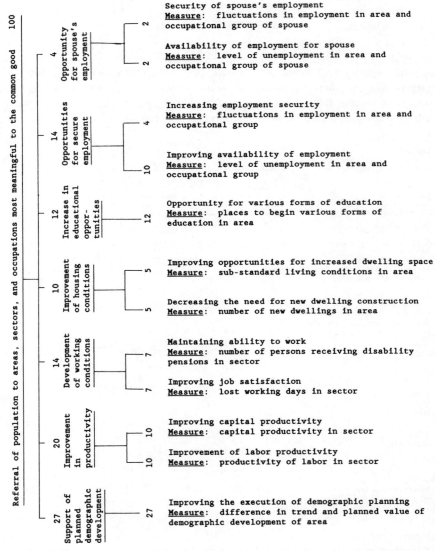

Figure 7.12
A Weighted-Ends Tree

The targets and means, in the sense understood by this coordinative method, are normally different kinds of activities. They may, therefore, be conceived of as entities. The criteria by which the states of means and ends are measured (indicated by "measure" in Figure 7.12) correspond to the variables. The links in most cases are obviously influence relations. On the other hand, a relevance tree may be interpreted as some kind of hierarchy, because it shows how main targets are divided into subtargets, and how these in turn are divided into smaller subtargets. They are thus, according to our terminology, entity or variable hierarchies. Behind the coordinative method, there actually lies the idea that there is both a hierarchy of means and a hierarchy of ends, connected to each other by various links. They are interdependent.

CONTINGENCY ANALYSIS

Contingency analysis was probably first introduced by Andrews and Muhlhan (1943) and was further developed by Osgood (1959). A text initially is divided into recorded units, according to relevant criteria. These recorded units then are analyzed by means of a list of content categories. The coder records the presence or absence of the relevant content category for each unit. The co-occurrences of categories within the same units are then computed and tested for significance against zero. Finally, the patterns of the nonrandom contingencies are analyzed.

Contingency analysis calculates the number of occurrences from a raw data matrix. This means that the method studies the coexistence relation without paying any attention to the actual type of relation. It thus counts all relations, regardless of whether they are influence, definition, inclusiveness, or other types. Contingency analysis therefore may be regarded as a rather simple form of syntactic method.

The matrices of contingency analysis are compilations similar to networks. The rows and columns, instead of nodes, stand for entities, and the intersections, instead of arrows, represent relations among these entities.

EVALUATIVE ASSERTION ANALYSIS

The general purpose of *evaluative assertion analysis* is to extract from a text the evaluations relative to certain concepts. The method was developed by Osgood and his colleagues (Osgood, Saporta, and Nunnally 1954).

SUMMARY

The syntactic methods reviewed in this chapter are based on four different syntactical patterns of thought or syntactic theories: the linguistic, logical, associative, and graph-theory approaches. We therefore have organized the methods into four main groups, each of which operates with a rather similar set of

	TERM RELATION	VALUE	VALUE RELATION (CAUSE-EFFECT)	VARIABLE	VARIABLE RELATION (INFLUENCE RELATION)	ENTITY	ENTITY RELATION	TERM MODEL	VALUE MODEL	VARIABLE MODEL	ENTITY MODEL	SEMANTIC APPROACH
LINGUISTIC METHODS												
LINGUISTIC-SYNTACTIC METHOD												
SYNTACTIC GRAPH	element graph											
SEMANTIC NETWORK		adjective	conjunction	noun	verb	noun	verb	tree diagram			network	part of network
LINKED MEMBER TABLE		adjective noun		noun		linked member	link	graph			matrix	
METHODS BASED ON PROPOSITION CALCULUS												
PROPOSITION CALCULUS		property	implication			entity	relation					
DISCURSIVE CONTENT ANALYSIS		property	relation			object			network			
N-SIM METHODS		sentence	syntax word						N-SIM matrix			
PICTURING METHOD		attribute	functional connectional			object	connection	picture	picture	picture	picture	hierarchic picture
METHODS BASED ON THEORY OF GRAPHS												
SIGNED DIGRAPH TECHNIQUE				variable	graph					graph		
COGNITIVE MAPPING				concept	causal belief link					cognitive map		
PSYCHOLOGIC						thinglike element	desirability relation					
ISM		attribute	relation	efficiency indicator	link	target means	relation link			relevance tree	network matrix tree	tree
COORDINATIVE METHODS												
METHOD FOR TARGET PROGRAMMES												
ASSOCIATIVE METHODS												
CONTINGENCY ANALYSIS						content category	coexistence				contingency matrix	
EVALUATIVE ASSERTION METHOD		common meaning material				value object			profile			

Figure 7.13

concepts. In addition to this, however, individual methods differ from each other with respect to details, as may be seen from Figure 7.13.

REFERENCES

Abelson, R. P., and M. J. Rosenberg. (1958). Symbolic psychologic: A model for attitudinal cognition. *Behavioral Science* 3: 1–13.

Allen, L. E. (1965). Sketch of a proposed semiautomatic, hierarchical, openended storage and retrieval system for statute oriented legal literature. In *Proceedings of the 1965 congress of the International Federation of Documentation,* Washington, D.C., pp. 189–98.

Andrews, T. G., and G. Muhlhan. (1943). Analysis of congruent idea patterns as a study in personality. *Character and Personality* 12: 101–10.

Axelrod, R. M. (1976). Decision for neoimperialism: The liberation of the British committee in 1918. In *The structure of decision,* ed. R. M. Axelrod., pp. 27–35. Princeton: Princeton University Press.

Carter, R. M. (1975). Elementary ideas of systems applied to problem solution strategies. In *Conference proceedings of the Society for General Systems Research* July 13–18, San Francisco, pp. 36–43.

Enkvist, N. E. (1975). *Tekstilingvistiikan perusk sitteitä.* Helsinki: Gaudeamus.

Farris, D. R., and A. P. Sage. (1975). On the use of interpretative structural modeling to obtain models of worth assessment. *Computer and Electronic Engineering* 2 (2): 149–74.

Hart, J. (1976). Analysis of nonmonofonic relations. In *The structure of decision,* ed. R. M. Axelrod. Princeton: Princeton University Press.

Klir, J., and M. Valach. (1967). *Cybernetic modelling.* London: Iliffe Books.

Krippendorf, K. (1969). Models of messages: Three prototypes. In *The analysis of communication content,* ed. G. Gerbner, 69–106. New York: John Wiley and Sons.

Kuusi, O. (1978). *A coordinative method for social policy target programs.* Helsinki: Publications of the Office of the Prime Minister.

Lyons, J. (1972). Generative syntax. In *New horizons in linguistics,* J. Lyons, 115–39. New York: Penguin.

Osgood C. E. (1959). The representational model and relevant research methods. In *Trends in content analysis,* ed. I. Pool. Urbana: University of Illinois Press.

Osgood, C. E., S. Saporta, and J. C. Nunnally. (1954). Evaluative assertion analysis. *Litera* (Istanbul) 3: 47–102.

Pietilä, K. (1975). *A study in the methodology of consciousness research.* Helsinki: Tampere.

Roberts, F. S. (1971). Signed digraphs and the growing demand for energy. *Environment and Planning* 3: 395–410.

Sigurd, B. (1974). Experiment med text. *Papers from Institute of Linguistics.* Stockholm: University of Stockholm.

Warfield, J. N. (1976). *Societal systems: Planning, policy and complexity.* New York: John Wiley and Sons.

8

Semantic Analysis

Of the two branches of the content analysis method, the semantic one is possibly the more significant, even though both semantics and syntactics are also important. The usefulness of the syntactic part depends on the skill with which semantic methods are employed. It is difficult, if not impossible, to build a network or other model from influence relations found in an analysis if the concepts are ambiguous. The attempt will succeed only if the concepts first are carefully standardized. This chapter introduces some applications of semantic methods.

In the preceding chapters, values of states were combined into variables, and variables and entities were combined into superconcepts and hierarchies in an attempt to find their common properties. In the opposite direction, superconcepts were divided into subconcepts by identifying properties that distinguish subconcepts from each other. Those procedures can be used to generate definitions, because the general idea behind forming them is that definitions consist of semantic components that describe the common or distinguishing properties of something. The process of definition is similar to the construction of variables from values and hierarchies from individual variables and entities. The concept to be defined is compared with concepts taken from the frame of reference that the manager has adopted. For each of these reference concepts, the conceptual or concrete world is divided into two parts, one to which the relevant concept belongs, and the other to which it does not belong. The range of relevant concepts is reduced by this form of exclusion.

In practice, the procedure is carried out by means of questions. Let us, for example, define the concept "human" (Figure 8.1). We will first define it according to systems theory by asking, Are we examining it as a term or a relation? If it is defined as a term, what kind of term is it? By these two questions, we exclude relations, variables, and values. We next proceed to concrete theory

INCLUDED		EXCLUDED
Does the concept "human" belong to terms?	No ▷	RELATION

Yes
▽
TERM

| Do we examine it as an entity, i.e. as a possessor of states and variables? | No ▷ | VALUE AND VARIABLE |

Yes
▽
ENTITY

| Does the entity have mass and occupy physical space? | No ▷ | ABSTRACT ENTITY E^1 |

Yes
▽
CONCRETE ENTITY E^1

| Is it capable of metabolism, growth, reaction to stimuli, and reproduction? | No ▷ | THING $E^{1.1}$ |

Yes
▽
BEING $E^{1.1}$

| Is it capable of spontaneous movement and rapid motoric response to stimulation? | No ▷ | PLANT $E^{1.1.1}$ |

Yes
▽
ANIMAL $E^{1.1.1}$

| Does it have a spinal column? | No ▷ | INVERTEBRATE $E^{1.1.1.1}$ |

Yes
▽
VERTEBRATE $E^{1.1.1.1}$

| How many legs does it have? | Four ▷ | QUADRUPED $E^{1.1.1.1.1}$ |

Two
▽
BIPED $E^{1.1.1.1.1}$

| Does it have pelage? | Yes ▷ | OTHER MANUAL $E^{1.1.1.1.1.1}$ |

No
▽
HUMAN $E^{1.1.1.1.1.1.1}$
=======

NOTE: The definition of a concept is formed by comparison with semantic components and thus finding its location in conceptual space.

Figure 8.1
Definition of a Concept

concepts by asking whether it is a concrete or an abstract entity, a being, or a thing. And so the analysis continues, until we have excluded all other concepts except the one we wish to define, that is, human.

DEFINITIONS

The definition of a concept is obtained by combining the answers to such questions. Each answer is one semantic component, and the definition is a string of such components. Each question in the process produces one or more semantic dimensions, which are termed *defining variables*. Each question thus establishes one or more defining variables, and the answers denote the values of the defined concepts in these defining variables.

The definition of the respective concept is obtained by combining the values of the defining variables (semantic components). It may be given briefly, laconically, by means of concept names, or, more thoroughly, by means of the definitions of these concepts. In short form, the definition of human reads according to Figure 8.1:

Human def)term & entity & . . . & biped & without pelage(.

In a more thorough form it is expressed as follows:

	possessor	has	occupies	capable		without
Human def)	of states and variables	& mass &	space	& of physical metabolism	& . . . &	pelage(.

The former is more economical but requires that the reader know what is understood by the defining concepts. The latter is heavier and far more complicated, but it is easier to understand.

The former is termed an *enumerating definition,* because it specifies the concept defined by enumerating all the concept categories belonging to it, from the broadest to the narrowest. The latter type is a *descriptive definition,* because it specifies the concept by describing the properties.

CONCEPTUAL SPACE

Concrete entities exist in spatiotemporal space, as discussed in the context of backdrops. Therefore, each concrete entity may be defined by means of its exact location at an exact moment in time. The location is specified by means of the three dimensions longitude, latitude, and altitude. Spatiotemporal space thus consists of these three dimensions together with time (Figure 8.2).

In a similar fashion, the defining concepts and their values form the conceptual space in which the concept is defined. The defining variables have the same

A)

Defined Concept	Defining Variables = Spatiotemporal Space			
	Location			Time
	Longitude	Latitude	Altitude	
Writer of this text	24° 51'	60° 20'	10 m	1991-11-12

B)

Concept Defined	Defining Variables = Conceptual Space					
	Concept Category	Term Category	Having Mass	Occupying Space	...	Values of Defining variables
Human	term	entity	yes	yes	...	
Ideology	term	entity	no	no	...	

NOTE: Entities in spatiotemporal space are identified by means of location and time (A). In conceptual space this is done by defining variables which the definers derive from their theoretical frames of reference.

Figure 8.2
Definitions in Spatiotemporal and Conceptual Space

role as longitude, latitude, altitude, and time in spatiotemporal space, but there is an essential difference. Whereas the defining variables in the spatiotemporal definitions are always the same and invariably limited to four, in conceptual space they vary according to the frame of reference the manager chooses to use. They are thus not constant. This means that their number can vary over a wide range. Sometimes only one or two variables are needed, and sometimes numerous defining variables are necessary. But the basic principle remains exactly the same. Each concept can be defined in table form analogous to the spatiotemporal definitions.

HIERARCHY, ENUMERATIVE, AND DESCRIPTIVE DEFINITIONS

In the context of our discussion of values, variables, and entities, hierarchies were constructed from the bottom up, beginning with concrete concepts and proceeding toward more abstract ones. In the defining process, we normally proceed in the opposite direction, since we move from broader concepts toward narrower ones. This means that the hierarchy is formed from the top, by writing the concepts included and excluded beneath the superconcept, as in Figure 8.3. Concrete entities are divided into beings and things, beings into animals and plants, and so on.

Each step in such a hierarchy is, in turn, regarded as a definition. "Real entities are beings and things," or "beings are animals and plants." It defines the superconcept by enumerating its subconcepts. Thus it is an enumerative definition. It may define the superconcept by enumerating its subconcepts exhaustively or merely by giving examples. The smallest conceivable hierarchy from which larger hierarchies can be constructed may be regarded as an element hierarchy.

Enumerative and descriptive definitions may be combined by writing the semantic components beneath a respective component, considering these semantic components as values of defining variables, and writing the relevant defining variables beside the hierarchy (Figure 8.3). In this way, one may simultaneously

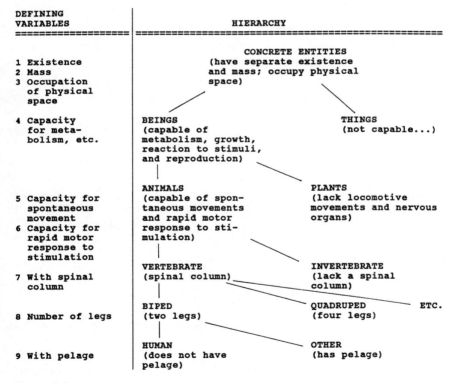

Figure 8.3
Definition Hierarchy Constructed from Top Down

organize the concepts into a hierarchy and define the concepts descriptively. From our perspective, this is an economical way of describing the conceptual space employed by a manager. It is, therefore, a fundamental part of the L-M theory approach to semantics.

STRUCTURE OF DESCRIPTIVE DEFINITIONS

A descriptive definition describes a concept by means of its properties. For example: "Fair performance is barely acceptable. It meets the minimal requirements, but falls short of the normal standards expected from a competent employee." Such descriptions are analyzed by dividing them into semantic components, representing the descriptive properties. These are "barely accepted," "meets the minimal requirements," "falls short of the normal standards," and "expected from a competent employee."

A descriptive definition consists of the following elements:

1. a defined concept, specified in the definition;
2. a defining concept, referring to the concept category to which the defined concept by definition belongs;
3. the values of the defining concepts, describing how the defined concept differs from other concepts included in the category of the defining concept; and
4. a definition relation, combining the defined concept with the defining concepts.

Accordingly, a descriptive definition in its general form reads: "Defined concept A belongs to the category of defining concept B and differs from other concepts in this category by having, in defining variable a, the value a_1, in defining variable b, the value b_1 . . . and in defining variable n, the value n_1." In terms of symbols, this is expressed as follows:

A def) B & a_1 & b_1 & . . . $ n_1 (or

$$\text{Concept def) to cate- and has property } a_1 \text{ and property } b_1 \ldots \text{ and property } n_1 \text{ (.}$$

belongs
Concept def) to cate- and has property a_1 and property b_1 . . . and property n_1 (.
gory B

For instance, the definition of "bachelor," often used as an example when introducing semantic methods, takes the following form:

	belongs	has in	in "age"	in "marital
Bachelor def)	to human &	variables	& value	& status" value (.
	beings	"sex" the	"adult"	"never
		value "male"		married"

ANALYSIS OF A DESCRIPTIVE DEFINITION

Descriptive definitions are analyzed by dividing the definition into semantic components, deriving defining variables from those components, and interpreting the semantic components as values of the defining variables. This takes place in two steps. The definition is first divided into components and then interpreted (presented by means of the components).

Text:
> "Fair refers to a performance level that meets the minimal requirements, but falls short of normal standards."

Concepts:
> "fair" = defined concept
> "refers" = definition relation
> "performance level" = defining concept, that is, "fair belongs to the category of performance levels"
> "meets the minimal requirements" = the value of a defining variable "meeting of minimal requirements"
> "falls short of normal standard" = the value of another defining variable, "meeting of normal standards"

Interpretation:

	performance	meets	falls short
Fair def)	level	& minimal	& of normal (
		requirements	standards

or " 'fair' belongs to the category of 'performance level' and differs from other performance levels in having the value 'meets' in the defining variable 'meeting of minimal standards,' and the value 'falls short' in the defining variable 'meeting of normal standards.' "

The definition can also be presented in the form of a table in which the defining variables are in columns (Figure 8.4). It furthermore can be described in the form of a starlike network in which one point indicates the defined concept, the other points are derived from the semantic components, and the middle location is occupied by the definition relation. This elementary network is shown in Figure 8.5.

DEFINED CONCEPT	DEFINING VARIABLES		
	Category to which defined concept belongs	Meeting of minimal standards	Meeting of normal standards
Fair	Perform- ance level	Meets	Falls short

Figure 8.4
A Definition Table

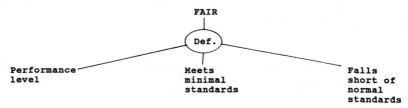

Figure 8.5
A Definition Elementary Network

COMBINATION INTO A NETWORK OF DEFINITIONS

When individual descriptive definitions are analyzed and presented in the form of an elementary network, they can be combined into a network of definitions, provided that they possess, pairwise, at least one concept in common. This may be exemplified by analyzing the vocabulary used in a set of concepts, a dictionary, a theory, or a book. By way of an example, a common vocabulary will be analyzed, beginning from the definition of "fair" as presented and analyzed above: "Fair refers to a performance level that meets the minimal requirements, but falls short of normal standards." In the next step, the semantic components of this definition are subjected to analysis. Thus, for instance, "performance" is defined as "an execution of a job" (Figure 8.6a). In this way,

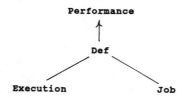

Figure 8.6a
Combining Elementary Networks

the analysis proceeds by subjecting everything to semantic analysis. The term *normal,* for instance, is defined as "expected from a competent employee" (Figure 8.6b).

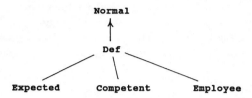

Figure 8.6b
Combining Elementary Networks

The analysis proceeds step by step, passing from the analysis of defined concepts to the analysis of defining concepts. At last the analyst reaches primitive concepts, those that are regarded as familiar to the audience, so that either they do not need to be defined at all, or they may be defined through some other primitive concept. To "execute," for instance, is defined as being able to "carry out," which in turn is defined as meaning to "put into effect," which is defined as meaning to "carry out" (Figure 8.6c). The ideas "to carry out" and "to put

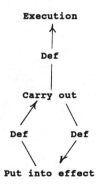

Figure 8.6c
Combining Elementary Networks

into effect" are primitive concepts of this kind, because the definer obviously thinks that the audience understands both of them.

When the whole set of concepts has been analyzed in this way, they can be combined into a network, provided they have at least one concept in common. This condition is naturally fulfilled in the step-by-step analysis described above, because the defining concepts of the one step are the defined concepts of the next, and thus pairwise in common.

Figure 8.7 represents such a network. The focal point or point of departure in this figure is the concept from which analysis begins (in our example, the term *fair*). The primitive or basic concepts are located at the periphery of the network. In Figure 8.7, each definition is identified by a set of numbers. The first number refers to the steps of the definition. Thus, definitions starting with a two belong to the second step, those with a three to the third, and so on. The second number

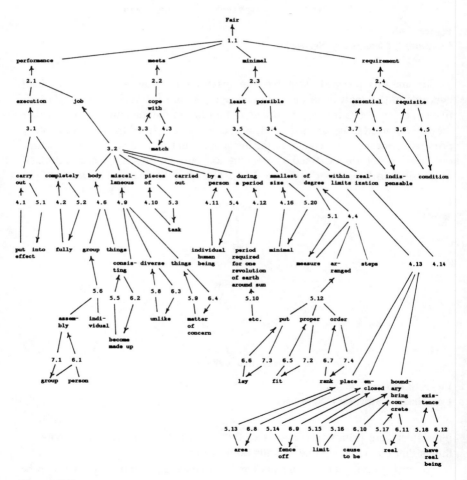

Figure 8.7
A Network of Definitions: A Compilation for Descriptive Definitions

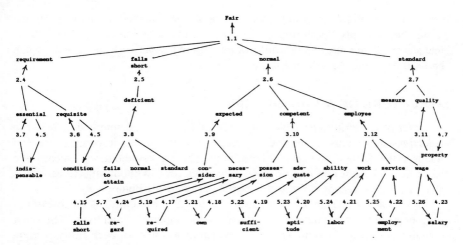

Figure 8.7 (continued)
A Network of Definitions: A Compilation for Descriptive Definitions

is an ordinal number referring to the definition within the respective set. Thus definition 4.14 is the fourteenth definition at the fourth level.

Normally, the chains of definitions involved in this network end with primitive concepts defined pairwise in relation to each other, as with, for instance, "to consider," defined as meaning "to regard" (5.7), and "to regard," defined in turn as meaning "to consider" (4.24). Or sometimes in the definition chain there occurs a concept that has already been defined, as is the case with "minimal" in definition 4.16, already defined by definition 2.3. Or sometimes the chain includes the concept that originally started the chain. This is the case with "falls short," which started the chain beginning with definition 2.5, and which occurs again as the defining concept of definition 4.15. When this happens, the definition has become circular.

USE OF DEFINITION NETWORKS

Definition networks like those in Figure 8.7 are less important than networks of propositions and hierarchies as compilations of enumerative definitions. But definition networks are sometimes useful for descriptions of the vocabularies of managers or procedure manuals, analysis of the logical consistency of a set of definitions, and collection of semantic components for their future treatment, such as formulation of definitions or verbal scales.

Networks are especially useful for applying scientific knowledge to management. Before any attempt is made to combine the conceptual sets of various scientific disciplines, their key concepts should be analyzed in this way. In this sense, the concepts "performance," "fair," "minimal requirement," and "normal standard" are interesting results of the Figure 8.7 network, because they can be used to formulate a verbal scale.

STRUCTURE OF A VOCABULARY

Descriptive definitions have some resemblance to the interaction between adjectives and nouns. Adjectives correspond to the semantic components and nouns to the defined concepts. A concept may be expressed either by means of a more general noun and one or more adjectives, or—without adjectives—by a specific noun referring only to this particular concept (Figure 8.8).

This means that there are two kinds of extreme vocabularies. One consists of only one noun—for example, an entity—and numerous adjectives. The other contains only nouns and no adjectives, which means that for each entity concept there is a separate noun. Each of these vocabularies has its advantages and drawbacks. An adjective vocabulary is far smaller than a noun vocabulary; most adjectives can be used in a great many contexts, and each context saves a noun. The disadvantage of an adjective vocabulary is that the sentences are very long. Each noun must be replaced by at least two or more words. The noun vocabulary is just the reverse, heavier in words but lighter in expression.

A large vocabulary and long sentences both require mental effort. A large vocabulary puts a great strain on the memory, and long sentences tax the capacity for verbal comprehension. Either extreme therefore, is impractical. For this reason, most languages have optimized or minimized mental effort, as shown in Figure 8.9. They rely on both a moderate number of nouns and a moderate adjective vocabulary.

In a similar way, descriptive definitions optimize mental effort. Adjectives can be replaced by descriptive definitions, further reducing the vocabulary, in the same way that nouns may be replaced by a more general noun plus adjectives.

Defined concept	Defining concept	Values of defining		
		Variable 1	Variable 2	Variable 3
More specific noun	More general noun	Adjective 1	Adjective 2	Adjective 3
Bachelor	Human being	Male	Adult	Unmarried

Figure 8.8
Vocabulary Structure

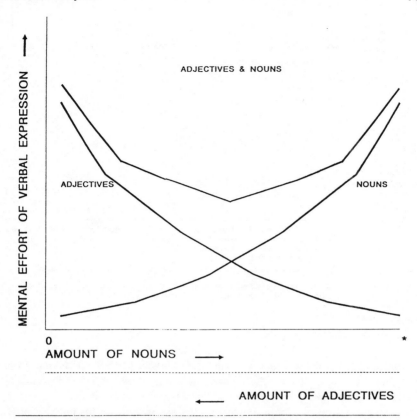

NOTE: An appropriate amount of adjectives and nouns minimizes the mental effort of verbal expression.

Figure 8.9
Minimum Mental Effort

But the language then becomes even more cumbersome. Let us merely think of replacing the word "beautiful" by the definition "property of an aggregate of qualities in a person or a thing that gives pleasure to the senses, especially in an aesthetic sense." It is obviously lighter to use "beautiful" instead of this definition.

EXPERTISE AND DEFINITION NETWORKS

The breadth of a definition network varies according to the expertise of the audience. The more acquainted they are with the subject, the smaller the network

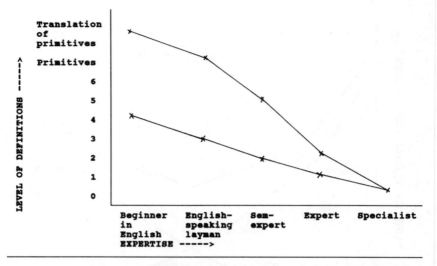

NOTE: The need for definitions decreases with increasing competence in the English language and the topic at hand.

Figure 8.10
Need for Definitions

is. Again consider the network of Figure 8.7. Those who are experts in personnel administration and, above all, in merit assessment generally understand as a matter of course what is meant by "fair" when it is used in the context of performance appraisal. Some, however, may ask what it means but are satisfied by a clue, that is, by the first definition, definition 1.1. But those who are not familiar with the jargon of personnel administration may, for instance, ask the meanings of "performance" or "minimal requirements." They require definitions at the second, third, and fourth levels. People who are not very competent in English may need further definitions and ask what is meant by "execution" or "job" in this context, which means that they need definitions at even the fifth or sixth levels. Finally, a beginner in English may not be satisfied even with the basic primitives, because he or she does not understand their meanings. They, therefore, must be translated into an understood language. Figure 8.10 graphs the relative needs for definitions.

COMPARISON OF CONCEPTS

Concepts found in an analysis often are rather vague. Sometimes they are defined ambiguously. Sometimes homonyms and synonyms are used.

Managers compare definitions with other definitions to discover differences and similarities. This comparison may be made in at least three ways, depending on the number of definitions to be compared: pairwise, when only two definitions are compared; in tabular form, when the number of definitions is less than ten; and by lists of defining concepts (semantic components), when comparing very many definitions.

In a pairwise comparison, definitions are written down one above the other in analyzed form so that values of the same defining variables fall into the same columns. Then the concepts in a column are compared with each other to determine whether they have the same meaning. An example is provided in Figure 8.11, where the definitions of "average" and "competent" are compared with each other. According to this comparison, they have the same meaning, except for the second defining variable, where "average" refers to existing performance level and "competent" to what is required.

In tabular comparison, the principle is exactly the same as in pairwise comparison, except that the columns of defining variables are provided with headings and respective questions, as shown in Figure 8.12. The definitions then are compared columnwise, as in the pairwise comparison.

When the number of definitions being compared is large, even a table is rather awkward. In such cases, it is appropriate to carry out the comparison by means of

DEFINED CONCEPT	DEFINING CONCEPT	DEFINING VARIABLES				
		1st	2nd	3rd	4th	5th
Average	Performance	which is	the mean	of persons	in the respective position	?
Competent	Performance	having	required	?	in the respective position	qualities (required)
Do they refer to the same concepts?	Yes!	Yes!	No! The first to what "is" and the second to what "ought" to be! ———— Difference	Yes! Even if the second only implicitly	Yes!	Yes! Even if the first only implicitly!

NOTE: The definitions are written down one above the other so that the semantic components belonging to the same defining variables fall in the same columns.

Figure 8.11
A Pairwise Comparison of Definitions

PERFORMANCE LEVEL		CONNECTED BY APPRAISAL	DEFINING VARIABLES					CONNECTED BY RESPONSE (SANCTIONS)			EXAMPLES OF SUBCONCEPTS OF STRONYMS
			CONNECTED BY COMPARISON WITH OBJECTIVES			CONNECTED BY IDEAL	CONNECTED BY MOTIVATION				
VERBAL	NUMERIC	ACCEPTANCE	MINIMUM OBJECTIVES	AVERAGE OBJECTIVES	TOP OBJECTIVES	NEED FOR IMPROVEMENT	ROLE AS EXAMPLE	VERBAL	PAY	TRANSFER	
SUBMARGINAL	1	Not accepted	Falls short	Falls short	Falls short	Too great	Hopelessly bad example for others	Makes comments and urges improvement		Immediate need for transfer to less demanding position (demotion)	Failure / Defective / Unfit / Disqualified / Rejected
FAIR	2	Barely accepted	Meets	Falls short	Falls short	Great need but hope and time for improving	Bad example	Improving; reminders and reprimands if repeated on purpose etc.	Entitled to no bonuses or merit pay raises	Gradual demotion considered if repeated	Deficient / Mediocre / Incompetent / Inadequate / Low quality
SATISFACTORY	3	Accepted without reservation	Exceeds	Meets	Falls short	Some need	Good example for beginners	Self-evident performance and no need for blame or recognition	Entitled to average bonus and to moderate merit pay raise if repeated	No need for promotion or demotion	Average / Sufficient / Adequate / Competent
GOOD	4	Accepted readily	Exceeds	Exceeds	Falls short	Only perfectionist improvement possible	Good example for average performers	Due for recognition if repeated	Entitled to high bonus or to considerable merit pay raise if repeated	Leads to promotion if repeated	Ample / Competent / Eminent / Pretty Good
EXCELLENT	5	Accepted with admiring surprise	Exceeds	Exceeds	Meets	Outsider cannot find any room for improvement	Hopelessly good example for average performers	Due for public recognition if repeated	Entitled to exceptionally high bonus and to significant pay raise if repeated	Leads to prompt promotion (provided there are openings)	Distinguished / Conspicuous / Appreciated / Ideal from viewpoint of management / Prominent / Striking / Gee whizz

NOTE: Each step in a verbal scale is represented by one or more descriptive definitions and one or more enumerative definitions.

Figure 8.12
Tabular Comparison

lists of defining concepts and variables. This means that each column in the comparison table is replaced by a list. The following lists are taken from Figure 8.12.

Defining Concepts
Performance
Performance level
Results
Person
Quality of Performance Criteria
Specific
Qualities
Consequences
Requirements
    Requirements
    Standards
    Objectives
"Level" of Requirements
    Minimum level
    Average
    Top performance
Relation to the Requirements: Positiveness
    Fails to meet
    Meets
    Exceeds

The comparison is carried out in the same way as in pairwise and table form comparisons. The question is asked of each list, Do its concepts refer to the subject or have the same meaning?

STANDARDIZATION

As the lists of defining concepts and variables increase in length, the definitions of the analyzed concepts are increasingly different, even if the words in each list are supposed to refer to the same concept. If the words in each list have different meanings, the concepts refer to different things. This often may be the case, even if the concepts are meant to refer to the same thing. Figure 8.13 is an example of this. Six different definitions of content analysis are analyzed. With

Definition to be analyzed	Definition concepts							
	Activity		Object of the activity		Method used in the activity		Performer of the activity	
	Name	Variables & values	Name	Variables	Name	Variables	Name	Variables
	a	ap	o	op	m	mp	p	pp
Content analysis is the statistical semantics of political discourse (Kaplan)	1 Semantics	1/1 Statistical	1 Discourse	1/1 Political				
Content analysis is any technique for making inferences by objectively and systematically identifying specified characteristics of message (Stone)	2 Making inferences 3 Identifying	2/1 Objectively 3/1 Systematically	2 Characteristics of message	2/1 Specified	1 Technique	1/1 Any		
Content analysis may be defined as referring to any technique for classification of sign vehicles which relies solely upon judgments ..of an analyst.. provided that the judgments are regarded as the report of scientific observer. (Janis)	4 Classification	4/1 Relies upon judgments	3 Sign vehicles		1 Technique	1/1 Any	1 Analyst	1/1 Regarded as a scientific observer
Content analysis is a research technique for the objective, systematic and quantitative description of the manifest communication. (Berelson)	5 Description	2/1 Objective 3/1 Systematic 5/1 Quantitative	4 Communication	3/1 Manifest	1 Technique	2/1 Research		
We propose to use the terms "content analysis"... to refer to the objective, systematic and quantitative description of any symbolic behavior (Cartwright)	5 Description	2/1 Objective 3/1 Systematic 5/1 Quantitative	5 Symbolic behavior	2/2 Any				
The term "content analysis" is used here to mean the scientific analysis of communications messages.... The method is broadly speaking the "scientific method" and while being catholic in nature it requires that the analysis be rigorous and systematic (Barcus)	6 Analysis	6/1 Scientific	6 Communications messages		2 Method	3/1 Scientific 4/1 Rigorous 5/1 Systematic		

Figure 8.13
Comparison of Various Definitions of Content Analysis

146

respect to the first two defining variables, "activity" and "object of the activity," almost all definitions seem to define content analysis differently.

In most cases, a manager can use only one definition for operational purposes. This means that a particular definition should be formulated on the basis of lists or columns of defining variables. The first step is to choose which defining variables are to be used in the definition. Then, if the lists of defining variables contain synonyms, one should decide which of them will be used or whether to resort to a quite new concept. If the words in the lists have different meanings, one or two of these should be selected and the others excluded. A definition thus formulated is termed a *standardized definition*. Figure 8.14 illustrates this procedure. It consists of two steps:

I. *Choice of Defining Concept and Values of Defining Variables*

Defining Concept	Performance level
Quality of Performance	Objectives
Reality of Performance	Actual compared with objectives
Level of Objectives	(1) Average performance
	(2) Top performance
Verb	(1) Meets
	(2) Fails to meet
Ratee	Persons in the respective job
Setter of Objectives	Employer

1. Choice of the name of the defined concept from the parallel synonymous names (in Figure 8.14: satisfactory).
2. Replacement of synonymous defining concepts by one standardized name (level of actual performance)
3. Selection of defining variables for the final definition (quality of performance criteria, reality of performance, level of objectives, verb, ratee, and setter of objectives), and
4. Selection of values for these variables (objectives, actual performance compared with objectives, average and top level, persons in relevant job, and employer).

II. *Formulation of the Standardized Definition*

"Satisfactory refers to the level of actual performance that meets the average level but fails to meet the top level in objectives set by the employer for persons in the respective job." In this way the concept names and their definitions can be made uniform.

ANALYZED CONCEPT	RESPECTIVE DEFINITION	DEFINING CONCEPT — Does it in this connection describe performance level?	DEFINING VARIABLES					
			QUALITY What type of performance level?	REALITY Existing, required, imagined or what performance level?	LEVEL OF REQUIREMENTS How demanding level?	POSITIVENESS Does the actual performance meet the requirements	RATEE Whose performance?	SETTER OF THE REQUIREMENTS Who has set the respective requirements?
ADEQUATE	Performance which is sufficient for a specific requirement	Yes = "performance"	"for a specific" requirement	"sufficient for requirement" = actual compared with required	(not specified)	"is sufficient"	?	?
AVERAGE	A level of performance which is average for persons in respective position	"level of performance"	(not specified)	"level of performance mean... = actual	"average of persons in the respective position	"is"	"persons in respective position"	?
COMPETENT	Performance which has qualities required by superiors	"performance"	"qualities"	"has qualities required" = actual compared with the required	?	"has"	?	superiors
EFFECTIVE	Performance productive of desired consequences	"performance"	"productive in consequences"	"productive in required consequences = actual/required	?	"is"	?	?
REJECT	Results deprived of the minimal qualities required	"results"	"minimal qualities"	"results deprived of minimal qualities"	"minimal"	"deprived"	?	?
SATIS-FACTORY	Performance conforming to standards for an average employee	"performance"	"standards"	"conforming to the standards" = actual/required	"average employee"	"conforming"	?	?
SUFFICI-ENT	Performance which meets objectives set for average employee	"performance"	"objectives"	"performance meets objectives" = actual/required	"average employee"	"meets"	?	?
Do they refer to the same concepts?		Yes! Performance or its results	Yes! Specific, qualities, requirements consequences, standards, objectives	Yes! Actual compared with the required	No! Average or minimal	No! Sufficient, is, has conforming, meets/deprived	Yes? Persons in respective position	Yes? Superiors
Standardization: Which concepts to be chosen for the standard definition		Performance level	Objectives	Actual/objectives	Average top	meets fails to meet	persons in the respective job	Employer

STANDARDIZED DEFINITION

Satisfactory refers to an actual performance which meets the average level but fails to meet the level in objectives se by the employer for persons in the respective job.

Figure 8.14
A Standardized Definition

148

A COMPLETE DEFINITION

A good definition is, from the user's point of view, comprehensive. The concept should be defined both descriptively and enumeratively. A descriptively comprehensive definition specifies the concept with regard to all defining variables relevant to a user's interests. An enumeratively comprehensive definition locates the concept in a hierarchy by specifying its superconcepts. To illustrate, we continue our example of performance criteria. A specialist in personnel administration will examine job performance from many descriptive angles. The angles could, for instance, include:

1. Appraisal, whether the results or the performance are acceptable.
2. Comparison with an ideal performance, to what extent there is room for improvement in the performance examined.
3. Comparison with objectives set by the employer, to what extent the performance meets the minimum, average, and top levels of objectives.
4. Response to which the performance is entitled, what kind of verbal, monetary, or promotional sanctions the performance merits.

The definition of "fair performance" thus takes the form presented in Figure 8.15.

"Fair refers to a performance that is

- barely accepted,
- meets the minimum requirements but falls short of the average level,
- within objectives,
- set by the employer,
- for persons in the respective job or position,
- entitled to a reprimand."

The enumerative refinement involves the category to which the concept belongs, its parallel concepts belonging to the same superconcept category, and its subconcepts or synonyms. In our example "fair," for instance,

1. Fair is one of the different performance levels (superconcept: performance level).
2. Other levels are submarginal, satisfactory, good, and excellent (parallel concepts).
3. Fair is used for words such as deficient, mediocre, incompetent, or inadequate (subconcepts or synonyms).

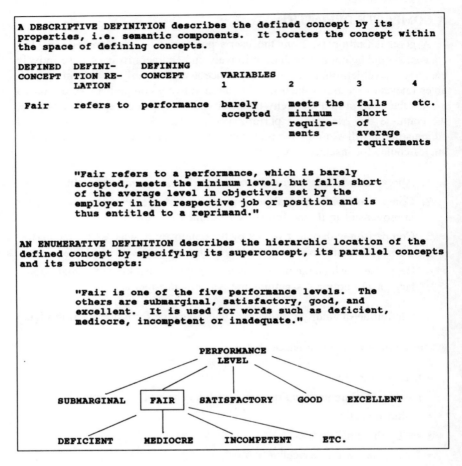

A **DESCRIPTIVE DEFINITION** describes the defined concept by its properties, i.e. semantic components. It locates the concept within the space of defining concepts.

DEFINED CONCEPT	DEFINI- TION RE- LATION	DEFINING CONCEPT	VARIABLES 1	2	3	4
Fair	refers to	performance	barely accepted	meets the minimum require- ments	falls short of average requirements	etc.

"Fair refers to a performance, which is barely accepted, meets the minimum level, but falls short of the average level in objectives set by the employer in the respective job or position and is thus entitled to a reprimand."

AN **ENUMERATIVE DEFINITION** describes the hierarchic location of the defined concept by specifying its superconcept, its parallel concepts and its subconcepts:

"Fair is one of the five performance levels. The others are submarginal, satisfactory, good, and excellent. It is used for words such as deficient, mediocre, incompetent or inadequate."

PERFORMANCE LEVEL

SUBMARGINAL   FAIR   SATISFACTORY   GOOD   EXCELLENT

DEFICIENT   MEDIOCRE   INCOMPETENT   ETC.

Figure 8.15
A Refined Definition, Defining the Concept Both Descriptively and Enumeratively

FORMULATION OF A VERBAL SCALE

Managers often define verbally the values of a variable or the steps of "a scale" (an assessment). From our point of view, each step may be seen as a definition consisting of both a descriptive and an enumerative part. This means that, in order to formulate a verbal scale, it is necessary to define the relevant steps in the manner already introduced.

When constructing a verbal scale, it is important to define the various steps by means of the same defining variables, so that the logic of the scale may be retained. The descriptive formulation is completed according to the following steps:

1. Choice of defining variables.

2. Choice of values to be used in each variable.

3. Formulation of definitions of each step by means of the values of the defining variables.

The enumerative definition is also formulated in three steps:

1. Naming the defining concept that will be the variable on which the scale will be formulated (performance level in Figure 8.15).

2. Assigning names and possible number values for each step (submarginal 1, fair 2, satisfactory 3, and so on).

3. Giving examples of concept names that are interpreted as belonging to each step (examples in Figure 8.15).

ANALYSIS OF A VERBAL SCALE

The same idea also may be applied to the analysis of verbal scales. In this type of analysis, the procedure is exactly the same as in synthesis. The analysis begins

The scale to be analyzed: "WORKING CONDITIONS" p^1		Measurable variables		
		p^2 FREQUENCY	p^3 DISAGREEABLENESS	p^4 NUMBER OF FEATURES
Degr.	Degree definitions			
A1 $p1$	Work performed under ordinary working conditions, involving slightly disagreeable features from time to time, or infrequent exposure to moderately disagreeable working conditions	p^2 from time 1 to time p^2 infrequent 2 exposure	p^3 slightly 1 disagreeable p^3 moderately 2 disagreeable	p^4 some 1 p^4 " 1
B p^1 2	Frequent exposure to moderately disagreeable working conditions	p^2 frequent 3	p^3 " 2	p^4 " 1
C p^1	Frequent exposure to definitely disagreeable working conditions	p^2 " 3	p^3 definitely 3 disagreeable	p^4 " 1
D p^1	Fairly continuous exposure to definitely disagreeable working conditions	p^2 fairly 4 continuous	p^3 " 3	p^4 " 1
E p^1	Fairly continuous exposure to highly disagreeable working conditions	p^2 " 4	p^3 highly 4 disagreeable	p^4 " 1
F p^1 6	Continual exposure to extremely disagreeable working conditions	p^2 continual 5	p^3 extremely 5 disagreeable	p^4 " 1

Figure 8.16
Analysis of a Verbal Scale

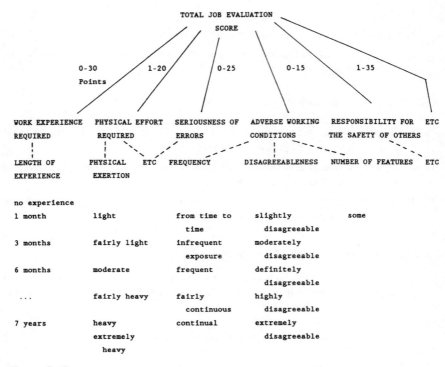

Figure 8.17
Analysis Results of a Verbal Scale in the Form of a Variable and Value Model

with descriptions of steps—by dividing them into semantic components, by locating the respective defining concepts and their values, and by presenting them in tabular form, as in Figure 8.16, or in a value model, as in Figure 8.17.

Figure 8.16 analyzes a scale that measures "working conditions." The first step, i.e., the "mildest" conditions, is specified by means of two definitions: "work performed under ordinary working conditions, involving some slightly disagreeable features from time to time" or "infrequent exposure to moderately disagreeable work conditions." The former is analyzed as having the following content:

Step 1 def) from time to   & some & disagreeable (.
             time (exposure)   conditions

Three defining variables are thus involved in the definition. The "frequency of exposure" having the value "from time to time," the "disagreeableness of features" having the value "slightly disagreeable," and the "number of features" having the value "some." The analysis table is formulated from these defining variables. Each variable is allotted a column, and the definitions of scale classes are on the horizontal lines. When a scale has been analyzed in this way, a manager obtains from the columns all the values occurring in the definitions of scale classes.

Sometimes the assessment system to be analyzed consists of several factors, each with a verbal scale. The analyst then describes the whole system as a combined model of variables and values, as Figure 8.17 illustrates. All the factors involved in the job evaluation system are presented by means of a variable model. Examples of factors are "work experience required," "seriousness of errors," and "adverse working conditions." Each of the factors is given zero to thirty-five points. The defining variables also are entered in the model, as indicated by the broken lines. Beneath each of the defining variables are the relevant values, the verbal scales. This format provides a short and compact description of the whole system of evaluation.

SUMMARY

The usefulness of syntactic analysis depends on the quality of semantic analysis. This chapter, consequently, provides detailed means for semantically analyzing communications in organizations. The fundamental procedures developed in the previous chapters are applied to developing clear and concise definitions of concepts. Such definitions are the stuff that comprises the communications that may be examined with the syntactical methods, and indeed with L-M theory, discussed in Chapter 7. The following chapter provides an overview of some semantic methods developed by various individuals.

9

An Overview of Some Semantic Methods

Chapter 8 provided examples of how semantic analysis may be accomplished. Semantic analysis is fundamental to syntactic analysis, consequently, it is important to identify procedures that may be fairly easy for managers in different organizations to use. The strength of analyzing the content of organizational communications is determined to a large extent by managers' expertise in semantics. This chapter provides several semantic analysis procedures.

BRIEF REVIEW OF SEMANTIC THINKING

The semantic ideas introduced in the preceding chapters are bipartite. They include descriptive thinking on the one hand, and hierarchic thinking on the other (Figure 9.1).

Descriptive definitions locate concepts in conceptual space and describe them by means of semantic dimensions termed *defining variables*. Conceptual space consists of these semantic dimensions. In semantic analysis, the descriptive definitions are divided into semantic components of the defining variables. When these individual definitions have been analyzed, they are combined into networks of definitions. This aspect of semantic analysis is suitable for the scrutiny, standardization, and synthesis of concept definitions and also of verbal scales.

Hierarchic thinking gives rise to enumerative definitions, describing how concepts are divided into subconcepts or combined into superconcepts. Individual enumerative definitions are conceived of as elementary hierarchies and may, therefore, be combined into broader hierarchies. Such hierarchic thinking permits the abstraction of observations, the operationalization of theoretical schemes, the construction of practicable applications from research results and theories, and the change of aggregate level (transition from macrolevels to microlevels, or vice versa).

```
┌─────────────────────────────────────────────────────────────────┐
│  1.  Descriptive Definitions locate concepts in the conceptual    │
│      space consisting of defining variables (semantic             │
│      dimensions)                                                  │
│                                                                   │
│          11.  Descriptive definitions are divided into semantic   │
│               components (values of defining variables)           │
│                                                                   │
│          12.  Individual definitions are combined into networks   │
│               of definitions                                      │
│                                                                   │
│                    Applications e.g.:                             │
│                    Analysis and formulation of concept definitions│
│                    Standardization of concept definitions         │
│                    Analysis and formulation of verbal scales      │
│                                                                   │
│  2.  Enumerative (hierarchic) definitions divide the concepts     │
│      into subconcepts or combine them into superconcepts          │
│                                                                   │
│          21.  Enumerative definitions are divided into subconcepts│
│          22.  Hierarchies:  individual definitions are combined   │
│               into hierarchies.                                   │
│                                                                   │
│                    Applications e.g.:                             │
│                    Abstraction                                    │
│                    Operationalization                             │
│                    Application                                    │
│                    Change of aggregate level (micro - macro)      │
│                                                                   │
│  3.  Combination of descriptive and hierarchic thinking           │
│                                                                   │
│          31.  Provision of hierarchies with descriptive definitions│
│               (i.e. criteria of combination or division)          │
│                                                                   │
│          32.  Provision of hierarchies with verbal scales         │
└─────────────────────────────────────────────────────────────────┘
```

Figure 9.1
Semantic Thinking In a Nutshell

These two parts are combined in many ways. A suitable method for defining concepts entails first describing properties by means of a descriptive definition and then exemplifying that definition by means of an enumerative definition. The respective descriptive definitions are combined with the concept hierarchies by writing the criteria for combining concepts into superconcepts or dividing concepts into subconcepts under the concept names in the hierarchy. In this way, the reader receives information about the organization of concepts in relation to each other and their definitions. Furthermore, various hierarchies may produce verbal scales, if the steps of verbal scales are regarded as descriptive definitions.

MEANING

Before examining particular semantic methods, a few words about the concept *meaning* are in order, since semantics is often defined as the study of meanings. In this sense, it covers a rather wide range of phenomena. There is thus some justification in claiming that almost all branches of the behavioral sciences are, in one way or another, interested in semantic problems, even if linguists are conventionally regarded as the indisputable experts in the subject. The scope of semantics extends from psychology through social psychology and linguistics to logic. This is apparent, for example, in the different species of meaning subjected to analysis within semantics. As presented by Leech, semantics is interested in seven different ingredients of meaning (1974). They are briefly summarized here, where they are compared in the context of the example given in Figure 9.2.

1. *Conceptual meaning* sometimes is also called denotative or cognitive meaning. This refers to the thing that the concept (word or symbol) under examination represents. In other words, conceptual meaning enumerates the conditions a thing must meet before the respective concept (word, name, and so on) can be applied. For instance, the conceptual definition of the word *woman* may be human, female, and adult. We attach primary importance in this book to this species of meaning, which also may be called logical or lexical.

2. *Connotative meaning* refers to other meanings of a concept or expression, over and above its purely conceptual one. Connotative meaning describes certain essential properties generally possessed by the concept under examination. These are not defining but describing characteristics. If the word *woman* is defined conceptually by the three features human, female, and adult, these three properties provide the criteria for the correct usage of that word. They thus are defining concepts. But there are a multitude of additional, nondefining properties that we have come to expect a referent of woman to possess. These include such things as "hard working," "experienced in cookery," or "prone to tears." They are examples of connotative meanings.

Conceptual definitions are unambiguous, whereas connotative ones are ambiguous. A concept that fulfills the conditions human, female, adult can always be called woman, but a concept that fulfills the conditions "hardworking, experienced in cookery, and prone to tears" cannot necessarily be termed woman because it sometimes fits girls, boys, and men.

3. *Stylistic meaning* refers to the social circumstances surrounding the usage of the word. For instance, some words or pronunciations, which we recognize as dialectal, tell us something of the geographical or social origins of the speaker, and certain other words refer to their "status scale of usage," meaning, for example, a range descending from formal and literary English at one extreme to slang at the other. Thus, for instance, the words *woman* and *broad* (in certain contexts) both refer to human, female, and adult, and thus have the same conceptual meaning, but the former is included in general usage and the latter in low-style slang. They have different stylistic meanings.

4. *Affective meanings* reflect the personal feelings connected with an expression. These include the attitudes of speakers toward listeners, or the feelings an expression arouses in a listener. The affective meaning depends on many

DEFINING VARIABLES	DEFINED CONCEPTS				
	Woman	Lady	Mrs.	Broad	Mother
Conceptual					
species	human	human	human	human	human
sex	female	female	female	female	female
marital status	0	0	married	0	normally married
children	0	0	0	0	has children
Connotative					
experience in cookery	experienced in cookery	experienced in cookery	0	0	experienced in cookery
proneness to tears	prone to tears	represses emotions	prone to tears	not prone to tears	prone to tears
Stylistic					
style	general	general	general	low-style slang	general
formality	0	0	formal	informal	0
Affective					
admirableness	0	admirable	0	despised	admirable
respectability	0	respectable	0	disdained	respectable
Collocative					
use	0	0	when addressing a person	0	0
Associative					
hardness	0	"semi-hard"	0	hard	soft

Figure 9.2
Ingredients of Meaning

things: on the attitude of a listener toward a speaker, on personalities, on social circumstances, and the like. When we say that tyranny is disgusting, we actually show that, deep down, we connect the feeling of disgust with the word *tyranny*. In this way, we express affective meanings.

5. *Collocative meaning* consists of the associations a word acquires on account of the meanings of words tending to occur in its environment. The words *pretty* and *handsome* share a common ground in the meaning good-looking but may be distinguished by the range of nouns with which they are likely to co-occur. Saying that pretty can be used together with the words girl, flower, and village, but that handsome should be used with man, car, or computer, denotes the collocative meanings of these two words.

6. *Associative meaning* refers to the associations that a word or an expression arouses in us. This is occasionally rather difficult to distinguish from affective or stylistic meanings and sometimes is regarded as a blanket term for these two. For example, when we record our impressions of the word *bagpipes* by saying that they are good rather than bad, soft rather than hard, and active rather than passive, we are expressing some of the associations this word produces. Of the methods to be introduced in this chapter, Osgood's semantic differential obviously emphasizes these kinds of associative meanings.

7. *Thematic meaning* is communicated by the way a person organizes a message in terms of ordering, emphasis, and the like. For instance, an active statement often is felt to have a different meaning from its passive equivalent, although in conceptual content the two may seem the same. For instance, the sentence "Ms. Smith donated the first prize" answers the question "What did Ms. Smith donate?" whereas the sentence "The first prize was donated by Ms. Smith" answers an implicit question "Who donated the first prize?" That is, the sentence suggests that the reader knows who Ms. Smith is, perhaps through previous association. The different meanings of these two sentences lie in the range of thematic significance.

Some additional types of meaning in which concepts may differ include *reflected meaning* and the pair *intended/interpreted meanings*. Among all of these kinds of meaning, however, we will concentrate mainly on conceptual ones. From the point of view of the procedures used, which kind of meaning managers analyze is irrelevant. All types of meaning ingredients may be regarded as defining variables and thus may be treated in the manner suggested in the previous chapter.

GENERAL CHARACTERISTICS OF SEMANTIC METHODS

The term *semantic methods* refers here to the different ways of analyzing and expressing the meanings of words, phrases, and sentences. The literature contains a great many such methods, and the semantic theories underlying them vary accordingly. In the present chapter, some of these will be discussed in general terms, although selected ones will be more closely examined. On the one hand, only those methods will be studied that may be regarded as componential, in the same sense as the descriptive definition introduced in previous chapters. Accordingly, methods based on ideas other than the componential approach will not be considered. On the other hand, discussion will be limited to the meaning of individual concepts. Words and the meanings of phrases and sentences thus will be excluded from the examination. Furthermore, the review only concentrates on ideas where meanings are divided into components, and not on the relations between words and the external reality they describe, a subject also conventionally included in semantics. This means that we accept as plausible the hypothesis that all semantics finally may be reduced to components representing certain basic concepts, or the concepts derived from them, even if this assumption appears to some extent doubtful. This componential approach indeed is rejected by some semanticists (Lyons 1972). We nevertheless insist on the procedure, because such a simplification suffices for the purpose of practicable management applications.

COMPONENTIAL APPROACH

All approaches to the semantic analysis of natural languages are based on the insight that the meanings of lexical items, words, and phrases are not unanalyzable or undefinable wholes. Within the componential approach, this insight is made explicit essentially in two ways. The first is by componential analysis, where the meaning of a concept is explicitly defined in terms of semantic components. These components are not necessarily part of the vocabulary of the language itself but are systems theoretical elements. The second is based on postulates of signification, according to which the meaning of concepts is defined by a set of postulates such as "A boy is male" and "If x is a boy, then x is male." In other words, the meaning of concepts again is described by means of components, which are attributes involved in these postulates. On this occasion, however, they are words—items of natural language. Thus they share basically the same componential approach. From the viewpoint of systems theories, it is not crucial whether the components are theoretical or belong to the language itself.

In the following sections some componential methods are reviewed briefly and compared with the L-M theory approach. Not all of them are conventionally called semantic. The unorthodox methods include, for example, the definition of a set in set theory.

METHODS INTRODUCED

The methods introduced may be grouped into two main categories, according to the type of semantic components with which they operate. Methods operating with components of natural language include: meaning postulates (Carnap 1956), technique of shared features (Bendix 1966), semantic memory (Quillian, according to Transgaard 1975), semantic differential (Osgood, Suci, and Tannenbaum 1957), and set theory. Methods operating with theoretical components include: structural semantics (Greimas 1966), componential analysis (Katz and Fodor 1963), and generative transformational grammar (Chomsky 1965).

Each of these methods will be introduced briefly with an account of the basic idea by which the meanings of words and concepts are described. They then will be compared with the semantic ideas of L-M theory. Attention will be paid to features that, in the previous chapter, were claimed as the essential elements of a semantic method necessary for the purposes of systems thinking (Figure 9.1). Of each method introduced we therefore ask the following questions:

1. How does it treat descriptive definitions?
   (11) Does it resort to value or variable language? That is, does it employ semantic components, or does it combine them into defining variables?
   (12) Does it combine them into networks of definitions?
   (13) Does it express the definition relation explicitly?
2. Does it emphasize enumerative definitions?
   (21) Does it provide the manager with a method for analyzing enumerative definitions?
   (22) Does it deal with hierarchies? Does it combine individual definitions into hierarchies?
   (23) Does it deal explicitly with membership or part relations in the hierarchies?
3. Does it combine descriptive definitions with hierarchies?

MEANING POSTULATES

Meaning postulates or *semantic rules* may be introduced formally, for example, as Rudolf Carnap does (1956). According to this procedure, the meanings of words or expressions are described by *meaning terms*. Meaning terms are other words in the form of postulates that have the general form "if x is p (for example, boy), then x is q (for example, male)" or "p is q (boy is male)." Meaning postulates also may contain logical constants such as "and," "or," or "not." For instance, the meaning postulate of "bachelor" may take the following form:

1. Bachelor $\rightarrow$ adult, male, unmarried

Such individual definitions are elements of *definition chains*. A chain is formed when the words by which the meaning of the first word has been described are defined in turn by means of new meaning postulates, containing new words, and the new words again are defined by new postulates. For instance:

2. Adult → fully developed, mature

3. Fully developed → finished its natural growth.

TECHNIQUE OF SHARED FEATURES

Bendix developed a method for analyzing the meanings of verbs (1966). According to this method, meanings are described by properties termed *shared features*. These features are, for example, "A has B" and "A does not have B." A table is formed by which one can describe the meanings of different verbs with shared features and compare them with each other.

Although Bendix used his method for the analysis of verbs, the same idea may be applied to the semantic analysis of any concept. Thus, for instance, the comparison of some words close to *bachelor* takes the form shown in Figure 9.3. The columns indicate the shared features, and the rows identify the words with close meanings.

	A is male	A is female	A is grown up	A has never been married	A has been married	A has lost his spouse through death
A is a boy	x					
A is a bachelor	x		x			
A is a widow		x	x		x	x
A is a widower	x		x		x	x

Figure 9.3
Comparison of Words Close to Bachelor by Means of Shared Features

SEMANTIC MEMORY

According to Transgaard, Quillian developed a psychological model termed *semantic memory* (1975). It quite obviously is a componential approach. According to this model, the concepts (lexical items) are stored in the human mind in the form of such notions as "human being," "man," "woman," "bachelor," and "widower." These are organized by the memory into a *mental picture*. A mental picture is in fact a set of superconcepts and subconcepts in the form of a hierarchy (Figure 9.4). Each concept is defined by *attributes* such as "bipedal," "primate," "mammal," "male," and the like. These attributes are diagrammed laterally beside the respective concepts.

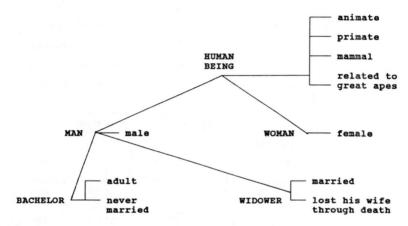

Figure 9.4
A Hierarchy of Concepts in the Semantic Memory of Quillian

SEMANTIC DIFFERENTIAL TECHNIQUE

Osgood, Suci, and Tannenbaum developed a method for describing the mental pictures people associate with words—for example, the associative meanings reviewed at the beginning of this chapter (1957). This method, called the *semantic differential technique,* is fairly well known within political science and sociology.

According to this technique, associative meanings are described by means of certain *semantic dimensions* (Figure 9.5). Each dimension is formed by two bipolar, antonymous adjectives such as "weak—strong" and "good—bad." Each of these pairs is provided with a scale of seven, five, or three classes, for example:

Happy ———:———:———:———:——— Sad

The person whose associations are being studied marks one of the categories, depending on how close the word being examined (for example, *polite* or *eager*) seems to the ends of the scale.

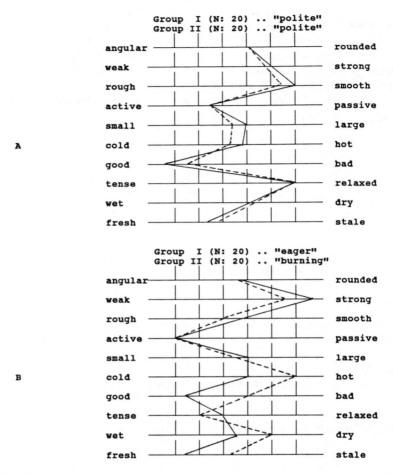

Figure 9.5
Semantic Profiles of the Semantic Differential Technique

All the semantic dimensions used in a single test together form the particular *semantic space* in which the meanings of words or concepts are measured. Through this semantic space, the results then may be described by means of *semantic profiles,* as in Figure 9.5, showing the profiles of the words *polite, eager,* and *burning* on the basis of answers by groups of test subjects.

The semantic dimension also may be formed by adjectives not regarded as the opposite ends of a continuum but as dichotomous. The dimension may then be constructed from either two or three classes in the following way:

	Male = +	Male = −
	or	and
	Female = −	Irrelevant = 0
		and
		Female = +

When each of these semantic dimensions is allotted a column, a table is formed that may be used for the description of meanings and associations of words subjected to analysis. Osgood has used this method to analyze the meanings of verbs (1970). When this table is applied to our example of words, it may take the form shown in Figure 9.6.

	Male-Female	Adult-Child	Married-Unmarried	Has lost spouse-Has not	Through death-Through divorce
Boy	+	−	0	0	0
Bachelor	+	+	−	0	0
Husband	+	+	+	−	0
Widow	−	+	+	+	+
Divorcee	+/−	+	+	+	−

Figure 9.6
Comparison of Words Close to Bachelor by Means of Semantic Differential Technique

SET THEORY

According to set theory, the concept of a set refers to any collection of individuals that are described as its elements. A set is defined in two ways. One way consists of naming all its elements, that is, saying that "set A is a collection of elements $a_1, a_2, \ldots, a_n$" and symbolized by

$A = a_1, a_2, \ldots, a_n.$

This is quite obviously an enumerative definition. The elements correspond to the subconcepts of an enumerative definition, and the set itself is their superconcept. It thus may be interpreted as an elementary hierarchy (Figure 9.7).

The other way a set may be described is by *specifying the properties* of the elements, that is by the definition written as "set A consists of all the elements a that satisfy the properties $P_1, P_2, \ldots, P_n.$"

This definition obviously represents the componential approach. If the set is regarded as the defined concept and the properties as semantic components, it is really a componential definition. Thus, for instance, "bachelor" may be defined as a set in the following way: " 'bachelor' is the set of human beings with the properties 'male', 'adult', . . . 'unmarried'." In symbolic form it is

Bachelor $=$ human being : "human being" has properties "male," "adult," . . . , "unmarried".

Set theory may be regarded as consisting of a componential semantic approach as well as of an enumerative semantic one.

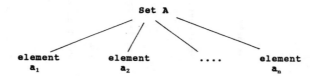

Figure 9.7
A Set as an Elementary Hierarchy

STRUCTURAL SEMANTICS

Structural semanticists believe the roots of componential analysis are in anthropology and therefore in structural semantics (Greimas 1966; Kuusi 1976). Structural semantics is grounded on a few basic concepts. According to these, the meaning of a word, sentence, or the like (known as *sememes*) is described by means of units called *semes*. A seme is defined as the smallest unit containing meaning. Normally, it is a single word such as "male" or "maleness," or "adult" or "adultness."

By means of semes, one may analyze the meanings of sememes and describe the differences of concepts close to their meanings. This analysis may be made in the form of a table (Figure 9.8). The plus sign indicates that the property described by the seme belongs to the sememe that is subject to analysis, whereas the minus sign shows that the seme does not describe the sememe. This approach is similar to the semantic differential approach. There are, however, two essential differences. First, a pair of semes in structural semantics, such as "adultness" and "adolescence," is replaced in the semantic deferential method by one semantic dimension, "adult-child." Second, there is no expression for irrelevance in structural semantics. Structural semantics thus operates in value language, whereas the semantic differential technique operates in variable language.

In another school among structuralists, represented by Levi-Strauss, a seme refers to an elementary dimension formed by two oppositional adjectives or expressions termed *lexemes* (1963). These are similar to those used in semantic differential technique. Two words are said to be oppositional if they can replace each other in a sentence without the sentence becoming meaningless. For instance, "adult" and "adolescent" are an oppositional pair and form the seme "adult-adolescent." This approach operates in variable language and is, there-

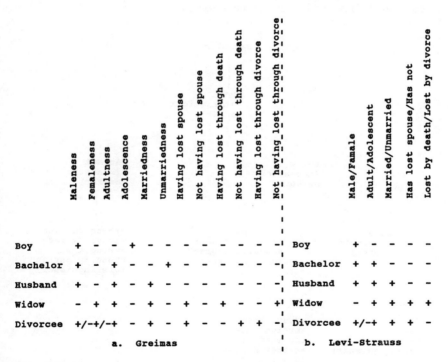

a. Greimas

	Maleness	Femaleness	Adultness	Adolescence	Marriedness	Unmarriedness	Having lost spouse	Not having lost spouse	Having lost through death	Not having lost through death	Having lost through divorce	Not having lost through divorce
Boy	+	-	-	+	-	-	-	-	-	-	-	-
Bachelor	+	-	+	-	-	+	-	-	-	-	-	-
Husband	+	-	+	-	+	-	-	-	-	-	-	-
Widow	-	+	+	-	+	-	+	-	+	-	-	+
Divorcee	+/-	+/-	+/-	-	+	-	+	-	-	-	+	+

b. Levi-Strauss

	Male/Female	Adult/Adolescent	Married/Unmarried	Has lost spouse/Has not	Lost by death/Lost by divorce
Boy	+	-	-	-	-
Bachelor	+	+	-	-	-
Husband	+	+	+	-	-
Widow	-	+	+	+	+
Divorcee	+/-	+	+	+	-

Figure 9.8
Structuralist Interpretations of Sememes Close to Bachelor

fore, similar to the semantic differential approach, except that there is no expression for irrelevance.

COMPONENTIAL ANALYSIS

The approach of componential analysis emphasizes the linguistic theories developed by Katz and Fodor (1963) and others. These theories define the meaning of a lexical element, normally a word, explicitly in terms of two sets of semantic components, markers and distinguishers.

Markers, on the one hand, may not be part of the vocabulary of the language itself but rather theoretical elements postulated to describe the syntactic role of a word under examination. These markers, termed *grammatical markers,* include, for example, "noun," "verb," and "adjective." On the other hand, markers may also express the semantic relations between the lexical elements of a given language. These markers, termed *semantic markers,* are the systematically chosen and standardized elements of the language, such as the sex antonym ("female-male") or the human-animal antonym.

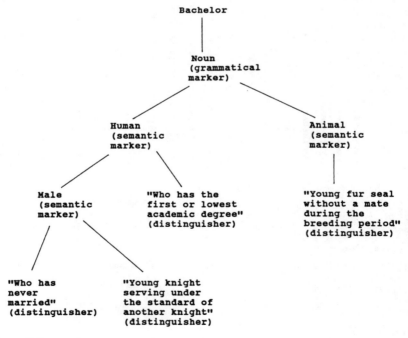

Figure 9.9
A Semantic Hierarchy for Presenting Meanings of Markers and Distinguishers

Distinguishers are unsystematically chosen words or phrases. Examples of distinguishers are "never marked" or "has the lowest academic degree."

In componential analysis, the meanings of lexical elements are described by means of markers and distinguishers connected by logical constants termed *conjunctions*. For example:

Bachelor: noun and human and male and unmarried

Adult: adjective and fully developed and mature

By means of these markers and distinguishers, the different dictionary meanings of a word may be presented in the form of a semantic hierarchy (Figure 9.9). Figure 9.9 gives four different meanings for the word *bachelor*.

GENERATIVE TRANSFORMATIONAL GRAMMAR

The semantic method presented by Chomsky (1965) in his generative transformational grammar is based mainly on the ideas of Katz and Fodor. According to Chomsky, the meaning of a lexical item is specified by means of a string of categories of features. *Categories* are grammatical characteristics such as "noun" and "adjective," and features are the real properties of the lexical item such as "human" and "adult." If a word belongs to the category of "nouns," it is denoted by "+noun," and if it does not possess the property of being animate, the relevant expression is "−animate." In this way, the meanings of words are expressed by means of strings of the following form:

Bachelor: +noun, +count, +human, +common, +adult, . . .

SEMANTIC METHODS COMPARED FROM THE VIEWPOINT OF L-M THEORY

How the various semantic procedures compare is important. Figure 9.10 provides a tabular comparison based on the concepts they employ. In the following paragraphs, we briefly discuss the various procedures in the context of systems thinking outlined in Figure 9.1.

(1.1) *Values or variable components.* Does a method deal with semantic components as valuelike concepts or combine them into semantic dimensions, representing variable language? The various methods actually represent three levels in this sense. Four of them (meaning postulates, semantic memory, set theory, and componential analysis) operate with plain, valuelike semantic components. Three of them (technique of shared features, structural semantics, and generative transformational grammar) form a nominal two- or three-step variable

METHOD	SEMANTIC COMPONENT (e.g. adult or adolescent)	SEMANTIC DIMENSION (e.g. age)	RELATION (e.g. is defined to be ...)	DESCRIPTIVE DEFINITION (e.g. bachelor is defined as an adult. ...)	COMPILATION OF DESCRIPTIVE DEFINITIONS (Not works of definitions)	ENUMERATIVE DEFINITION (e.g. Mr. A and Mr. B are bachelors)	TREE (HIERARCHY) (COMPILATION OF ENUMERATIVE DEFINITIONS)
MEANING POSTULATES	meaning term		----->	meaning postulate semantic rule	chain of definitions	no	no
TECHNIQUE OF SHARED FEATURES	shared feature			(implicitly)	no	no	no
SEMANTIC MEMORY	attribute			mental picture	no	no	mental picture
SEMANTIC DIFFERENTIAL	antonymous adjectives: class	semantic dimension		semantic profile	no	no	no
THEORY OF SETS	property			specification of a set by its properties	no	specification of a set by its elements	no

	value of defining variable	defining variable	definition relation	descriptive definition (of a concept)	networks of definitions	enumerative definition	concept hierarchy
STRUCTURAL SEMANTICS Greimas	seme			(implicitly)	no	no	no
STRUCTURALIST SEMANTICS Levi-Strauss	lexeme	seme		(implicitly)	no	no	no
COMPONENTIAL ANALYSIS	marker	distinguisher		(implicitly)	chain of definitions	no	semantic hierarchy
GENERATIVE TRANSFORMATIONAL GRAMMAR	category	feature		string of categories and features	chain of definitions	no	no
L-H THEORY	value of defining variable	defining variable	definition relation	descriptive definition (of a concept)	networks of definitions	enumerative definition	concept hierarchy

Figure 9.10
Comparison of Semantic Methods by Means of the Concepts They Employ

171

from these valuelike semantic components. Such a scale, for instance, constructed from the semantic component "adult" takes the form of +adult ("is adult"), −adult ("is not adult"), and 0 ("adult is not relevant to the defined concept"). Two of them (semantic differential and the structural semantics of Levi-Strauss) employ semantic dimensions; that is, they operate with variable language. In both cases, these variables consist of two oppositional adjectives, such as "hot" and "cold" or "old" and "adolescent" with various numbers of steps between them. The variables are nominal, although they could be interval or even ratio-variables, such as "temperature" or "age."

Incorporating variable language makes a method more useful. In Figure 9.8, for instance, twelve columns are needed in conjunction with valuelike components (*a* part), but only five are needed when variables (*b* part) are used. Furthermore, variable language allows a manager to write down, word for word, the expressions found in a definition. This has two advantages compared with plus-minus techniques. On the one hand, it saves the original expressions, but it is also more intelligible than symbolic + or − expressions. We may, therefore, regard variable language as more economical, more useful, and more mature in this respect.

(1.2) *Networks of definitions*. Three methods combine the individual definitions into large compilations that resemble networks of definitions. They are Meaning Postulates, Componential Analysis, and Generative Transformational Grammar. The other six methods do not offer any compilations.

(1.3) *Explicit expression of definition relation*. None of the methods reviewed pay explicit attention to the connection between the defined concept and the semantic components. In four of them, however, the definition relation is allotted a symbol of its own: the method meaning postulates symbolizes the definition relation by an arrow, set theory denotes it by an equal sign, and componential analysis and generative transformational grammar refer to it by a colon.

(2.1) *Analysis of enumerative definitions*. Only one of the methods reviewed, set theory, provides managers with a method of expressing enumerative definitions. The others make no reference to them.

(2.2) *Hierarchies*. Two of the methods employ some kind of hierarchy. Semantic memory uses a mental picture and componential analysis uses a semantic hierarchy or tree.

(2.3) *Explicit expression of part or membership relations*. None of the methods have any direct reference to these relations. Semantic memory and componential analysis nevertheless symbolize these relations in their hierarchies by means of lines.

(3) *Combination of descriptive definitions with hierarchies*. The only method that does this is semantic memory. Combining descriptive definitions in a hierarchy is important because it shows how the concepts are divided into sub-

concepts or combined into superconcepts, but it also reveals by means of attributes the criteria used in hierarchic combination or division.

SEMANTIC METHOD ACCORDING TO THE
L-M THEORY SUMMARIZED

The semantic L-M theory approach introduced in the previous chapter is a combination of the methods reviewed and expressed in tabular form (Figure 9.10), except that the names have been standardized into logico-mathematical ones. Thus, for instance:

1. The semantic component is replaced by the value of the defining variable, instead of form of meaning, shared feature, and so on.
2. The semantical dimension or seme is replaced by the defining variable.
3. The definition relation is symbolized either by "^{def}" or an arrow for the purposes of network construction.
4. The mental picture or tree is replaced by the concept hierarchy.
5. The definition of sets by means of their elements is replaced by enumerative definitions.

But, as well as being a standardized summary of the methods reviewed, L-M theory is also supplemental. There are at least three principal additions:

1. L-M theory combines enumerative definitions into hierarchies and thus combines, for example, the ideas of semantic memory and set theory.
2. L-M theory combines defining variables and hierarchies by regarding the defining variables as criteria for the subdivision of the concepts included in a hierarchy. This synthesizes ideas from other componential semantic methods with the semantic memory method. It allows the simultaneous presentation of descriptive definitions and the hierarchic organization of relevant concepts, as illustrated in Figure 9.11.
3. L-M theory replaces plus-minus tables by verbally expressed semantic tables, making them applicable to all kinds of defining (semantic) variables, not only to dichotomous or trichotomous nominal scales, and improving the readability of the tables. According to this way of thinking, the meanings of closely related concepts may be presented in a tabular form analogous to the methods of structuralists, Bendix and Osgood, with each of the defining variables allotted a column but with the relevant values recorded verbally.

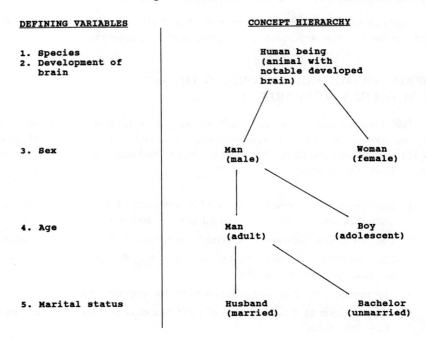

Figure 9.11
A Simultaneous Presentation of Descriptive Definitions and Hierarchic
Organization of Respective Concepts

SUMMARY

This chapter has surveyed several semantic methods used in various disciplines. The L-M theory method discussed in earlier chapters incorporates useful aspects of these methods. While managers may find a particular method well suited for a particular problem, we believe L-M theory better facilitates a comprehensive analysis and synthesis of organizational information into customized management theories.

REFERENCES

Bendix, E. H. (1966). Componential analysis of general vocabulary: The semantic structure of a set of verbs in english, hindi and japanese. *International Journal of Linguistics* 2.
Carnap, R. (1956). *Meaning and necessity*. Chicago: University of Chicago Press.
Chomsky, N. (1965). *Aspects of the theory of syntax*. Cambridge, Mass.: Massachusetts Institute of Technology Press.

Greimas, A. J. (1966). *Semantique structurales*. Paris: Larousse.

Katz, J., and J. Fodor. (1963, April–June). The structure of a semantic theory. *Language* 39: 170–210.

Kuusi, O. (1976). Merkkij rjestelm t strukturaalisen tutkimuksen kohteena. *Äidinkielen opettajien liiton vuosikirja* (Helsinki) 23: 11–24.

Leech, G. (1974). *Semantics*. New York: Penguin.

Levi-Strauss, C. (1963). *Structural anthropology*. New York: John Wiley and Sons.

Lyons, J. (1972). Introduction. In *New horizons in linguistics*, ed. J. Lyons. New York: Penguin.

Osgood, C. E. (1970). Interpersonal verbs and interpersonal behavior. In *Thought and language*, ed. J. L. Crowan, 133–226. Tucson: University of Arizona Press.

Osgood, C. E., G. J. Suci, and P. H. Tannenbaum. (1957). *The measurement of meaning*. Urbana, Ill.: University of Illinois Press.

Transgaard, H. (1957). *The cognitive component of studies and beliefs*, vol. 27. Helsinki: Socialforsknings Institutet.

10

Summary

The world is filled with management theories, and the management-theory-of-the-month club continues to crank them out. The last thing the world needs is another limited-scope theory proclaimed the panacea of all management problems. What the world almost certainly needs is a theory that allows managers to evolve customized management theories from the activities and communications of their own organizations. Management observation and communication theory does just that.

Most widely proclaimed management theories are outlines of how a particular management team managed in a particular successful situation over a particular period. By the time the team is willing to reveal its secrets, other teams have developed ways of countering its successes. Notwithstanding the highly used management theory market, successful managers succeed by exploiting advantages unique, or nearly unique, to their own organizations—not by forcing their organizations into a half worn-out scheme.

Sets of lofty objectives often are copied from other companies with little attention given to formally connecting them to the actual concrete processes occurring in an organization. A great gulf develops between what managers believe is occurring and what actually is occurring—between the sated goals of the organization and its purposes. Customized management theories should be developed by observing the concrete processes of organizations, determining what their purposes are, and identifying goals that serve those purposes. Management observation and communication theory provides a conceptual framework for doing that.

The conceptual frameworks we espouse for developing management observation and communication theory are James Grier Miller's living systems theory and Heikki Heiskanen's linguistic-mathematical theory. Living systems theory provides a concrete processes perspective, and L-M theory instructs the introduction of formal conceptual and abstracted systems.

LIVING SYSTEMS THEORY

Living systems theory attempts to define concrete structures and processes as unambiguously as possible. To the extent achievable with contemporary measurement technology, concrete processes should be measured. When that is not possible, they should be assessed through other observation methodologies.

Living systems theory views all existence from the perspective of living systems. From that perspective organizations are concrete living systems—higher-order human systems composed of identifiable subsystems and components. They incorporate various forms of matter, energy, and information transmissions, such as materials, people, electricity, and telephone messages.

Organizations have purposes and goals. Purposes are internal and goals are external. Organizations develop a preferential hierarchy of values of interrelationships and interactions among their components. Decision rules emerge from that hierarchy, determining an organization's preference for a particular dynamic steady state. That steady state is the organization's fundamental purpose. The complex of values is compared to information entering the organization in determining how that information is associated and how any related matter-energy elements are distributed. A fundamental purpose may be subdivided into multiple and simultaneous purposes. Organizations pursue external goals (often termed *objectives*) to satisfy their purposes. Both purposes and goals arise in the concrete processes of organizations and their physical environments. Determining and controlling purposes and goals and identifying the abstractions termed *objectives* is the management function.

L-M THEORY

L-M theory combines several methods and procedures for rearranging the information of the communications occurring within organizations. It is a general systems theory consisting of a collection of principles for dividing observations, research, and literature findings into elements and compiling those elements for linguistic and nonquantitative numeric assessments and mathematical, computational, and other treatments.

L-M theory centers on concepts, which are divided into basic concepts and auxiliary concepts. Basic concepts consist of categories of observations, and auxiliary concepts describe basic concepts. Basic concepts have two major classifications: terms and relations. Terms reference separately, distinctly existing objects and are subclassified as values, variables, and entities. Relations reference connections among separately existing objects. They connect terms and include such things as dissimilarities and influence. Auxiliary concepts are classified as either defining concepts or metaconcepts. Defining concepts define basic concepts, and metaconcepts relate basic concepts to each other. Distinguishing between the objects being described and the concepts describing them is important. The term *state* is used to distinguish an object from the term or entity describing it.

L-M theory uses two fundamental types of hierarchies, part hierarchies and membership hierarchies, to rearrange those concepts. Other compilations also are used, such as networks, stars, tables, and various symbolic notations. The rearrangements produce reports, scales, and assessment instruments.

The concepts of L-M theory are fundamental concepts common both to logic and to mathematics. Consequently, they can be used to integrate social science, computer science, statistics, and mathematics in accounting and management information systems. This is an important characteristic, because very narrow management problems can be solved with sophisticated mathematical methods, somewhat broader ones can be evaluated with simple mathematical methods, and a wide range may be investigated using qualitative (logical) methods. All three approaches are needed to solve the ever-changing problems confronted by managers.

L-M theory provides operational instructions on how to construct concept hierarchies and networks, operating with logico-mathematical concepts. It uses analytic methods to translate linguistic concepts into logico-mathematical ones, and vice versa. Such methods incorporate both syntactic methods, to show how factual statements may be broken down to discover their meaning, and semantic methods, to show how definitions can be broken into elements and compared with each other. Combination methods show how results of analyses may be combined into hierarchies and networks. Synthetic methods are used to show how new concepts can be produced by combining available concepts—incorporating both semantic methods—to compare concept definitions and formulate new ones, and syntactic methods, to formulate research findings and analyses into practical applications.

This book started with the cube of resource administration. We stated that mastering such complexity is extremely demanding—in fact, nearly an impossible job. Management observation and communication theory, however, is meant to make it easier. It involves a set of logico-mathematical concepts useful for formalizing everyday information and processing it into reports. Hierarchies enable the application of company philosophy to everyday activities and derive concrete objectives from a company's strategy. Networks and models are used to organize the chaotic complexity so that specialization and integration are possible.

We also introduced systems theoretical tools containing the methodological means for applying these logico-mathematical concepts, hierarchies, and models to practical situations. The tools may seem, from the viewpoint of practicing managers, far too complicated and difficult to be practicable. They must be simplified before managers can use them easily. Nevertheless, they are necessary.

Computers can be used to simplify the methods. Most of the systems theoretical tools can be provided in the form of interactive and paperless computer programs. Some of the work can be done by simple word-processing and calculus programs. But most of all, one needs tailored programs.

Some such programs already have been developed. Here are some examples:

- Prove It enables a manager to set the objectives for a firm and its organizational units just as precisely as desired and monitor how these objectives are achieved.

- Payday enables the manager to master the pay of his personnel and other areas of personnel administration.

- Weigh and See has been written to evaluate jobs and determine just and equal pay.

- Name the Game presents a company's philosophy or strategy in the form of sets, each consisting of some ten minicases, and analyzes whether the players have acted in accordance with the philosophy and strategy advocated.

- Answer Me analyzes survey results concerning, for example, personnel's opinions concerning company objectives, organizational climate, leadership style, and the like.

- How Am I Doing enables the self-analysis of one's own leadership style, personality, and the like.

These programs require that the user be familiar with methods in the methodological tool box only in a common-sensical way. For instance, in the area of semantics, the user must define what is meant by the objectives used. When abstracting, a manager must know the structure of the organization and how different objectives are tied to each other. The programs take care of the rest: calculate means, regressions, correlations, make compilations, and so on. Mainly, the user needs only to master the substance. The programs do the processing. They are built on the systems theoretical tools presented throughout this book and incorporate them.

BACKDROPS AND SOURCE SYSTEMS

A backdrop consists of the terms and their relationships that comprise communications about the individual observations and auxiliary concepts connecting them to a particular language or other conceptual system. The construction of backdrops focuses on terms, and the use of backdrops focuses on relations. Management observation and communications theory connects the construction and use of backdrops to specific observations of states of the concrete processes of organizations. That action ensures that the theories managers construct concern those processes. A particular observation is the starting place for constructing backdrops.

Managers use backdrops to build source systems. A source system consists of multiple observations and has a subject population, a subject topic, and a time period. Managers use source systems to study limited aspects of organizations. Such source systems are connected to the concrete processes of organizations by the multiple observations from which the backdrops are developed.

SYNTACTIC AND SEMANTIC METHODS

The book introduced several syntactic and semantic methods to illustrate that a wide range of procedures are available for applying management observation and communications theory to particular organizations. L-M theory itself contains syntactic and semantic procedures. We believe those procedures incorporate the best features of the many procedures available in the literature.

SUMMARY

The world is filled with management theories. The book has not attempted to add one more but rather to present a megatheory for constructing individual theories customized to the management of particular organizations. This megatheory is based on the commonality of linguistic and mathematical theories.

Nevertheless, this book does not propose that every organization use the particular L-M theory it presents, but does propose that concepts common to both language and mathematics be used to connect managers' dreams for the future to the concrete processes they manage. By doing so, the science of management will be advanced enhancing the propaedeutics of the art of management.

Index

Abstracted systems, 18
Abstract entities, 79–80
Aggregate hierarchy, 67, 69–71
Auxiliary concepts, 33

Backdrop, 34–35, 37–38, 51–93, 180–81
Basic concepts, 33

Causation, 92–93
Coexistence: coordinate system, 86–90; pair, 83–84; row, 85–86. *See* Covariation relations
Cognitive mapping, 119–21
Cognitive networks, 112–14
Combination principles, 100–104
Componential analysis, 168–69
Concepts: auxiliary, 33; basic, 33; comparison of, 142–45; logico-mathematical, 40–47
Conceptual space, 79, 131–32
Conceptual systems, 18
Concrete processes, 1–2
Concrete systems, 18
Content analysis, 105–109, 146
Contingency analysis, 125

Controlling, 17
Coordinative method for social policy target programs, 122–25
Covariation relations, 92–93. *See* Coexistence

Decider subsystem, 17
Definitions, 132–53; descriptive, 132–36; enumerative, 132–34; networks, 136–42; standardization of, 145–48
Disparity, 90–92
Discursive content analysis, 117

Elementary hierarchy, 33–37
Entity, 33–37, 66–73; language, 47–49; models, 98–99
Estimate, 58–59
Evaluative assertion analysis, 125
Exactness, 60–64
Exclusivity, 51–53
Exhaustive collections, 51–56

Functions, 24

Generality, 38
General systems theory, 8–9, 31–33, 38–40

Generative transformational grammar, 169
Goals, 2, 24

Hierarchy: aggregate, 67, 69–71; membership, 60–61, 65, 71–73; part, 60–61, 67; process, 71; theory, 9–11, 99–100
Human history, 24

Information, 25–27, 47–49; markers, 25; mathematical, 43–49; qualitative, 43–44, 46–49; quantitative, 43–44, 46–49; subsystems, 26
Integrative general theory, 11–13
Interpretation, 27–28
Interpretive structural modeling, 121–22

Language: entity, 47–49; value, 47–49; variable, 47–49
Lexemes, 167
Linguistic-mathematical (L-M) theory, 2, 6–9, 10–13, 31–50, 38–42, 106–109, 169–74, 178–80
Linguistic syntactic analysis, 110–11
Living systems, 18–29
Living systems theory (LST), 2–3, 10–11, 15–29, 38–40, 178
Logico-mathematical concepts, 40–47

Management, 17, 24–25; information, 25–26
Management art, 4–5
Management science, 4–5
Management theory, 1, 3–4, 15–16, 177–78
Mathematics, 43–49
Matter-energy subsystems, 26
Meaning, 156–59
Meaning postulates, 161–62
Measurement, 27–28, 58–59
Membership hierarchy, 60–61, 65
Metaconcepts, 35–37

Normalized sentence-index matrix (N-SIM technique), 117

Objective numbering, 40
Objectives, 1–2
Observation, 34, 56–58, 80–83
Organizations, 18–24, 76–77; partipotential, 18; totipotential, 18; source systems, 76–77

Part hierarchy, 60–61
Picturing method (PIX), 117–18
Precision, 60–64
Process, 23–24; hierarchy, 71
Propositional calculus, 115–17
Psychologic, 121
Purposes, 2, 24

Qualitative information, 43–44, 46–49. *See also* Information
Quantitative information, 43–44, 46–49. *See also* Information

Relations, 33–37

Semantic analysis, 129–75, 181
Semantic components, 35
Semantic memory, 162–65
Semantic networks, 112–14
Semes, 166
Set theory, 165–66
Signed digraph technique, 118–19
Simplification, 5–6
Source system, 75–77, 80, 180–81
Space: conceptual, 79–80, 131–32; spatiotemporal, 77–79
State, 34–37
Steady state, 18
Structural semantics, 166–68
Structure, 23–24
Subsystems, critical living, 19–23
Supporting variables, 78–80
Syntactic graphs, 111–12
Syntactics, 106–27, 181
System: abstracted, 18; conceptual, 18; concrete, 18; definition, 6, 18; living, 18; partipotential, 18; source, 75–77, 80, 180–81; totipotential, 18
Systems thinking, 6

Table of linked elements, 114–15
Technique of shared features,
  162
Terms, 33–37
Theory, Hierarchy of, 38–40

Value, 33–37, 51–55; language, 47–49
Variable, 33–37, 51–56, 64–66; lan-
  guage, 47–49; models, 97–98
Verbal scale, 150–53
Vocabulary, 140–41

About the Authors

HEIKKI HEISKANEN is a management consultant with clients mainly in the Scandinavian countries and the Eastern European nations. His scholarly works include publications of the Finnish Academy of Science, books and journal articles in the Finnish language. He has developed numerous professional manuals and computer programs to implement management observation and communication theory.

G. A. SWANSON is a Professor of Accounting at Tennessee Technological University. His more than 50 articles have appeared in such journals as *Systems Research, Behavioral Science, The Accounting Review, Internal Auditor, Advances in Accounting, Accounting Historians Journal,* and *The Journal of Business Education.* He is coauthor of *Measuring and Interpretation in Accounting— A Living Systems Theory Approach* (Quorum, 1989) and *Internal Auditing Theory—A Systems View* (Quorum, 1991).